TAAS
Preparation and Practice Book

McGraw-Hill Reading

TAAS
Preparation
and
Practice
Book

Table of Contents

Test-taking Tips

- **Always read the directions carefully before you begin your work.**

- **Read each story slowly and carefully.**

- **Check your understanding of the story as you read it.**

- **Read each question carefully. Say the question again in your own words if you do not think that you understand it.**

- **Read all the answer choices for each question.**

- **Eliminate wrong answers.**

- **Keep your mind on your work.**

Test-taking Tips

- **Take your time as you do your work.**

- **Enjoy what you are reading.**

- **If you finish your test and have extra time, go back and recheck your answer choices.**

- **Always answer all questions.**

- **Look for clues to the meaning of the underlined words.**

- **Questions that ask about a character's feelings are asking you to think about how the character would feel.**

Test-taking Tips

Tips for Filling in Bubbles

The TAAS reading test is computer-scored. This means that instead of your teacher correcting your test, a computer will correct it. The computer looks at the bubbles that you darkened in your test booklet.

Filling in these bubbles is easy, but there are some rules you need to follow to be sure that the computer reads your answers correctly.

- **Using a pencil, fill in each bubble completely. Fill in only one bubble for each question.**

- **If you make a mistake and need to change your answer, be sure to erase completely.**

- **Do not make any pencil marks near the black bars that run down the inside of the pages. Also, don't make any extra pencil marks too close to the answer bubbles.**

Correct	Incorrect	Incorrect	Incorrect	Incorrect
○ 2 ○ 5 ● 7 ○ 9	○ 2 ○ 5 ✗ 7 ○ 9	○ 2 ○ 5 ✓ 7 ○ 9	○ 2 ○ 5 ◎ 7 ○ 9	○ 2 ○ 5 ◑ 7 ○ 9

Directions: Read each story. Then read each question about the story. Choose the best answer to the question. Mark the space for the answer you have chosen.

SAMPLE

The Bike Ride

"Come on," said Andy. "Put your <u>helmet</u> on and make sure that it is buckled under your chin."

"I'm glad we can ride our bikes on this dirt road," said Matt.

Andy and Matt were visiting their Aunt Julia on her farm. They were spending two weeks of the summer with her.

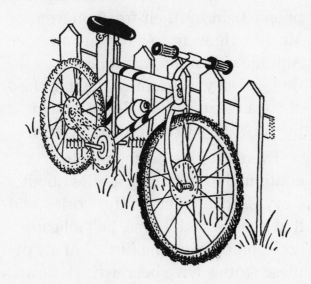

SD-1 The word <u>helmet</u> in this story is something you wear on your —

  ○ knees

  ○ feet

  ○ head

  ○ fingers

SD-2 Who were Andy and Matt visiting?

  ○ Their sister

  ○ An uncle

  ○ Their aunt

  ○ Their grandparents

STOP

Tall Tales and Truth about Davy Crockett

For over 200 years, people have told stories about Davy Crockett. One of the stories about him says that he killed a bear when he was only three years old. Another story tells about a time when he was fighting in a war. The other soldiers were chasing Davy. In order to get away, he jumped on the back of an alligator that he rode up a large waterfall.

While these stories are not true, Davy Crockett was a real person. He was a man who fought for the United States his entire life. Davy made many people laugh with his "tall tales" about his life.

Davy Crockett was born on a farm in Tennessee in 1786. He had five brothers and three sisters. His family was very poor. They got most of their food from hunting. Early in his life, Davy learned how to be a good hunter. He was glad he could help provide food for his family.

In 1798, Davy helped a man move his herd of cattle 400 miles to a different state. Davy was only twelve years old. He already knew a lot about the animals and the land that they lived on. Later, when Davy was twenty-seven, he fought in the army. He fought against the Creek Indians. During the Creek War, his wife Polly died. Davy left the army to take care of his children.

The people of Tennessee heard how brave Davy Crockett was in the war. They liked the funny stories he told about his life. Because they knew he was a good man, they voted for him to be their Congressman in Washington. Davy was delighted to serve as a member of Congress.

In Washington, Davy continued to fight for the people. He fought against a law that would make it hard for poor people to get land to farm. He was also against the idea of taking land away from the Indian tribes. He would say, "Just be sure you are right and then go ahead." It was important to him that the things that people did were good things.

In 1836, Davy left Washington and went to Texas. He wanted to help the people fight for their freedom from Mexico. He went to a fort in San Antonio called the Alamo. Even though Davy was a brave fighter, the Mexican Army killed all the men in the fort. Davy Crockett died a hero.

Even after his death, people continued to tell funny stories about Davy Crockett. One of the stories said that he was "half horse, half alligator, and a bit of snapping turtle." Many of these stories have been written down in books. People everywhere know the strange and somewhat true tales of Davy Crockett.

Go on

1 How did Davy Crockett probably feel about hunting for food for his family?

○ Angry

○ Confused

○ Proud

○ Tired

2 Before Davy Crockett fought against the Creek Indians, he —

○ went to the Alamo

○ became a Congressman in Washington

○ helped on a cattle drive

○ rode an alligator over a waterfall

3 Where was Davy Crockett born?

○ Texas

○ Tennessee

○ Washington

○ Maine

4 How did Davy Crockett feel about being a member of Congress?

○ Sad

○ Glad

○ Afraid

○ Disappointed

5 Which is a FACT in this story?

○ Davy Crockett once swam across the Mississippi River.

○ Davy Crockett traveled to California to hunt for gold.

○ Davy Crockett was in the army.

○ Davy Crockett's father ran an inn.

6 When does this story take place?

○ A long time ago

○ Yesterday

○ Sometime in the future

○ Last month

Go on

Zilker Pool Diving Contest

When Jeremy got home from school, he found a letter his mother had put on his bed. The letter was about a diving contest at the local pool. Jeremy read the letter twice to be sure he knew all about the diving contest.

After dinner, Jeremy talked with his parents about the letter. Jeremy had been diving since he had turned nine last summer and he was eager to be a part of the contest. He asked his parents for their help in picking dives for the contest. They said that his best two dives were the back flip and the swan dive.

Jeremy knew from the letter that he would have to sign up for the contest before the <u>deadline</u>. He would also need to practice his dives at the pool. He could hardly wait until the day of the big contest.

Zilker Pool Diving Contest
(Sign-up form on other side)

Ages	Diving Group
6 to 8	1
9 to 11	2

INSTRUCTIONS

1. Find the age group that includes your age. Check to see which Diving Group you will be in. Use the diving group number on the sign-up form.

2. On the form, list the dives that you will perform in the contest. You must do two dives.

3. A parent or guardian must sign the form before you turn it in.

4. Mail or bring the form to Zilker Pool by April 17. No forms will be accepted after the deadline.

SCHEDULE

May 25	9 A.M.	Arrive at pool and register
	10 A.M.	Begin first round of dives
	11 A.M.	End first round of dives
	1 P.M.	Diving show by Matt Scoggins
	2 P.M.	Begin second round of dives
	3 P.M.	End second round of dives
	4 P.M.	Winners will be announced

PRIZES

There will be one first place and one second place prize awarded in each diving group.

- First place winners will receive a trophy and a contest T-shirt.

- Second place winners will receive a red ribbon and a contest T-shirt.

- All others will receive a contest T-shirt.

Go on →

7 How did Jeremy feel when he found out about the diving contest?

   ○ unhappy

   ○ excited

   ○ confused

   ○ terrified

8 Jeremy chose to do a back flip and a swan dive because —

   ○ he could not do any other dives

   ○ his parents thought they were his best dives

   ○ his teacher said he should do them

   ○ the contest rules required those dives

9 The word <u>deadline</u> in this story means —

   ○ the last date something can be turned in

   ○ a letter describing a contest

   ○ a list of people who will be in a contest

   ○ the names of the winners

10 At what time will the diving show begin?

   ○ 11 A.M.

   ○ 1 P.M.

   ○ 2 P.M.

   ○ 4 P.M.

11 Before Jeremy talked to his parents, he —

   ○ won a trophy in the contest

   ○ practiced his best two dives

   ○ read the letter twice

   ○ watched a diving show by Matt Scoggins

Go on

Hopson Finds His Way

Hopson was a young kangaroo who was always looking for a faster way to travel. Usually, kangaroos hop across the plains. Their strong legs help them jump high and far. A powerful tail keeps them <u>balanced</u>, so they do not fall over. Hopson liked to hop, but he wanted to go faster.

One day as Hopson was hopping around, Erica Eagle flew over Hopson's head. She settled in a nearby tree.

Hopson asked, "How do you fly so fast?"

"I have large wings, and I always flap them very hard. When I take off, I leave from a high place so that I catch a lot of wind under my wings," answered Erica Eagle.

"I want to be able to move fast," said Hopson. He hopped over to a high pile of rocks and tried to jump up to the top. The sharp rocks scraped his front paws. "Ouch!" cried Hopson. He jumped down off the rocks and landed next to his Auntie Rooga.

"Eagles fly, kangaroos hop. Be a kangaroo," said Auntie Rooga to Hopson. Then she hopped swiftly across the plain.

Hopson was disappointed. He went down to the river. There he saw Cory Crocodile swimming. Cory Crocodile could swim very fast. Cory Crocodile swam past, moving his strong tail. Hopson had a strong tail, too. That gave him a great idea. Hopson hopped into the water. Instead of floating, his head went under the water and he came up, spitting water out of his mouth.Hopson shook the water out of his eyes and made his way to the shore.

Auntie Rooga stood on the bank and watched Hopson jump out of the river. He looked up at her sadly. "Crocodiles swim, kangaroos hop. Be a kangaroo," said Auntie Rooga to Hopson.

Hopson hopped back onto the plain. As he hopped, he saw the grass ahead of him move. Suddenly he saw Sandy Snake <u>slither</u> quickly through the grass.

"I can do that," thought Hopson. "I can crawl quickly on my belly like Sandy Snake does." Hopson lay down on his belly and tried to crawl through the grass. He could barely move as he dragged his big feet behind him.

Hopson rolled over and saw Auntie Rooga standing over him. She shook her head and said, "I wonder when Hopson will learn his lesson!"

Just then, Hopson saw lightning come from some big, dark clouds in the sky. Hopson and Auntie Rooga needed to get to shelter quickly.

Hopson popped up onto his big feet. He hopped very fast across the plain, while Auntie Rooga hopped right beside him.

When Hopson and Auntie Rooga reached the shelter of the forest, Auntie Rooga turned and smiled. "Hopson, you did not try to fly or to swim or to slither on the ground. You hopped!"

"Yes," said Hopson. "Eagles fly, crocodiles swim, and snakes slither on the ground. But I am a kangaroo. Kangaroos hop." Hopson had finally found the best way for him to move.

Go on

12 The main idea of this story is that Hopson —

- ○ has strong legs
- ○ learns the best way to move fast
- ○ talks to Auntie Rooga
- ○ wants to fly like an eagle

13 How did Auntie Rooga feel about Hopson at the end of the story?

- ○ Gloomy
- ○ Sad
- ○ Pleased
- ○ Angry

14 The word <u>balanced</u> in this story means —

- ○ sloppy
- ○ steady
- ○ fast
- ○ hungry

15 Which is a FACT in this story?

- ○ Erica Eagle flies with large wings.
- ○ Auntie Rooga does not know how to hop.
- ○ Hopson talks to a fish in the river.
- ○ A dog shows Hopson how to run.

16 In this story, the word <u>slither</u> means —

- ○ slide
- ○ fly
- ○ swim
- ○ hop

17 Which is the first animal that Hopson tries to be like?

- ○ Auntie Rooga
- ○ Cory Crocodile
- ○ Sandy Snake
- ○ Erica Eagle

18 What is this story mostly about?

- ○ Hopson tried other ways of moving but learned that the kangaroo way is the best way for him.
- ○ An eagle, a crocodile, and a snake showed Hopson how they move fast.
- ○ Hopson hopped into the forest to get out of the storm.
- ○ After he jumped into the river, Hopson came up spitting water.

19 How did Hopson feel after he tried to swim like Cory Crocodile?

- ○ Pleased
- ○ Curious
- ○ Happy
- ○ Disappointed

Go on

A Letter from Emily's Scout Leader

Emily could hardly wait until next weekend. Her Scout troop was going camping. She had to pack for the trip, but she was not sure what she needed to take.

That afternoon a letter came for Emily in the mail. It was from her Scout leader, and it was all about the camping trip.

Dear Emily,

I am looking forward to the camping trip we will be going on with our troop. I know the other girls are also excited. You must have questions about the trip. I have tried to answer them in this letter.

Who: All of the girls in Troops 65 and 82 will be going on this trip. In addition, several girls from Troop 78 in Waco will be joining us. These are girls who missed the camping trip that their own troop had last week.

Where: Our trip will be to Garner State Park. The park has a small river with some nice places to swim. We'll put up tents in a clearing near the river.

When: We will leave from the Trans' house at 4:30 on Friday afternoon. We will return at 5:00 on Sunday afternoon. Your parents should arrange to drop you off and to pick you up at the Trans' house.

How: We will be traveling by van to the park. Then we will carry our equipment in our backpacks about one mile to the campsite.

What to bring: Bring a sleeping bag, pillow, and extra blanket. It might be cold at night, and we will be sleeping on the ground. You must bring <u>necessities</u> such as a toothbrush, a tube of toothpaste, and a hairbrush. You do not have to bring a book to read, but you may if you would like to. You will need warm clothes to sleep in at night. During the day, shorts and a t-shirt should be warm enough.

Other: Your parents must complete and sign the permission slip. It is very important that they include all information that is asked for. You cannot go on this trip without the permission slip.

I am certain that this will be a great trip and am looking forward to seeing you on Friday. Please call me at home if you have any questions. My home number is 550-6221.

See you on Friday!

Mrs. Andrews
Scout Leader

Go on

20 The word <u>necessities</u> in this story means —

    ○ things you may not have

    ○ clothes to sleep in

    ○ things you need for the trip

    ○ a backpack to carry things

21 This story is mostly about —

    ○ a camping trip

    ○ a home phone number

    ○ a new Scout leader

    ○ permission slips

22 According to the letter, Emily does NOT have to bring —

    ○ a toothbrush

    ○ a book

    ○ a t-shirt

    ○ a sleeping bag

23 The Scout Leader's letter shows that she is —

    ○ preoccupied

    ○ unfriendly

    ○ helpful

    ○ confusing

24 Girls from Troop 78 in Waco will be going on the camping trip because —

    ○ they are good friends with the other girls

    ○ the Scout Leader wants them to join her troop

    ○ Emily asked them to come on the trip

    ○ they missed the camping trip for their troop

25 The Scout Leader sent the letter because —

    ○ she wanted to introduce herself

    ○ she wanted to answer Emily's questions

    ○ she wanted Emily's parents to go on the trip

    ○ she wanted to invite Emily to the zoo

26 At the beginning of the story, Emily feels —

    ○ curious

    ○ upset

    ○ sad

    ○ excited

Go on

Sarah's Trip to the Office

Sarah Herrera stood next to her mother on the elevator. They waited for the elevator to reach the eleventh floor. Since there was no school that day, Sarah was going to work with her mother. Sarah did not think the day would be fun. Finally, the elevator arrived. The door opened and Sarah looked around the reception area.

Even though Sarah had never been to her mother's office before, she just knew the day would be boring. She had made sure that she had brought a good book to read. As she walked down the hall beside her mother, Sarah looked into the rooms on either side. Most looked like offices. They were very plain and had desks with computers and phones on them. One room had a copy machine and another room had machines for sodas and snacks.

They eventually reached her mother's office.

"Well, what do you think?" her mother asked as Sarah inspected everything. Sarah smiled broadly at the impressive office. "You can put your backpack on the table beside the couch," her mother added. Sarah looked out the big window at the city below. They were up very high, so she could see a long way.

A few moments later, Sarah's mother said, "I would like a soda. Would you like something?"

"Sure," said Sarah. "But I can get it. I think that I saw the snack room as we were walking down the hall." Sarah was pleased with herself. She had been <u>observant</u>, so she knew just where to go.

Sarah turned left out of the office. She counted five doors until she reached the snack room.

Sarah used the money her mother had given her to buy two sodas from the machines along the wall. She also bought a candy bar for herself. She would eat it later. Sarah carefully carried the snacks back to her mother's office.

The people walking up and down the hall carried papers and books. Sarah could hear phones ringing and people talking in the offices along the hall. A man pushing a cart loaded with office supplies stepped aside to let her go by.

As Sarah set the sodas on her mother's desk she said, "There are almost as many people in the halls here as there are at school. What a busy place!"

Sarah's mother nodded in agreement. She was sorting through a stack of papers on her desk. "Sarah," she said, "would you like to help me make copies of these papers? I'll show you how to use the copy machine. And later today we can have lunch at the

Go on →

restaurant on the top floor of this building if you would like."

As they walked to the copy room, Sarah's mother introduced her to some of the other people who worked there. Sarah felt very grown-up as she shook hands with her mother's friends.

By the time they got back to her mother's office, Sarah was sure the day would be terrific. "Thanks, Mom," Sarah said. "I never knew there were so many fun things to do at work!"

---

27 Before Sarah bought sodas from the machine, she —
- ○ ate lunch at a restaurant
- ○ met her mother's friends
- ○ learned how to use the copy machine
- ○ got money from her mother

28 What is the main idea of this story?
- ○ Sarah gets to buy a candy bar.
- ○ Sarah learns that going to her mother's office is fun.
- ○ Sarah meets her mother's friends.
- ○ Sarah enjoys eating lunch at a restaurant.

29 In this story, the word <u>observant</u> means —
- ○ feeling sad
- ○ having fun
- ○ watching carefully
- ○ not paying attention

30 When Sarah first arrived on the eleventh floor, she felt —
- ○ bored
- ○ confused
- ○ angry
- ○ happy

31 Sarah felt grown-up because
- ○ she got a candy bar
- ○ she met her mother's friends
- ○ the office was high above the city
- ○ her mother's office was fun

32 Which of these is NOT a fact from the story?
- ○ Sarah met her mother's friends.
- ○ Sarah and her mother ate lunch outside.
- ○ The office had a snack machine.
- ○ There was a copy room on the eleventh floor.

Go on

Snowy Day Plans

Winter vacation was only two weeks away. Donna's father was planning to take Donna and her best friend Li to the mall. Li and Donna had always lived just down the street from one another.

The morning of the shopping trip, Donna looked out her bedroom window. During the night, a <u>blizzard</u> had covered the ground with deep snow.

Donna called Li on the phone. "Have you looked outside this morning?" Donna asked Li.

"Yes," said Li. "There is snow everywhere! The roads are covered with snow and the police have <u>recommended</u> that people not drive today. What are we going to do?"

"I guess we shouldn't go," said Donna. She thought of all the fun things that they had planned to do. They had wanted to buy gifts for their families for Valentine's Day. They had also wanted to play video games and to eat lunch at the food court.

"Maybe you can come over to my house today," said Li. "My mom can help us make cookies. Then we can watch a funny movie on television."

"That is a great idea!" exclaimed Donna. "I'll ask my parents if it is all right if I come over. I'll call you back in a few minutes."

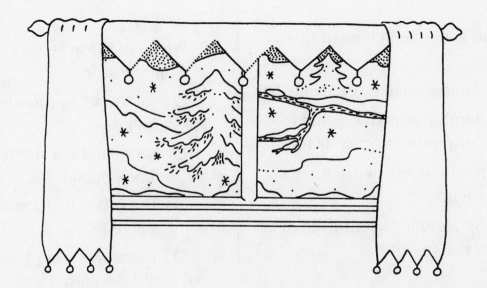

33 You can tell from this story that when something is <u>recommended</u>, you should —

    ○ go shopping

    ○ call a friend

    ○ do that thing

    ○ buy a present

34 The word <u>blizzard</u> in this story means —

    ○ a big snowstorm

    ○ a long car trip

    ○ a funny person

    ○ a hot wind

35 This story is mostly about —

    ○ going to a movie

    ○ baking cookies

    ○ changing plans they made for a shopping trip

    ○ playing video games at the mall

36 Which sentence tells something that is make-believe?

    ○ Donna talked to Li on the phone.

    ○ Snow covered the ground.

    ○ Donna and Li planned a trip to the mall.

    ○ A snowman said, "Come out and play!"

END OF PRETEST

STOP

Directions: Read the story. Then read each question about the story. Choose the best answer to the question. Mark the space for the answer you have chosen.

A Day at the Aquarium

Annie jumped out of bed and ran to wake up her mother. Today they were going to the aquarium. Annie hadn't been to the aquarium in a long time. More than anything else, she wanted to see the dolphins again.

The workers at the aquarium were busy getting ready for the show. They brought out big buckets of fish for the dolphins. Annie smiled at them. The workers waved at Annie and her mother.

Annie and her mother sat in the very first row. Annie wanted to be as close to the animals as she could be.

A man carrying a whistle came over to Annie's seat. "Are you here for the show?" he asked.

"Yes," Annie replied. "What is the sound that the dolphins are making?" she asked.

"That's how they talk to each other," the dolphin trainer explained. Then the man blew his whistle. The dolphins swam around the pool and jumped into the air. When they landed back in the water, they <u>drenched</u> the audience with water.

After the show, the man called one of the dolphins. The dolphin came right to the edge of the water. Annie got to see the dolphin up close. She even got to touch his nose! It was a very good day at the aquarium.

1 The word <u>drenched</u> in this story means —

   ○ soaked

   ○ swam

   ○ trained

   ○ waved

2 This story is mostly about —

   ○ a girl who visits the aquarium

   ○ dolphins eating fish

   ○ a class trip to the aquarium

   ○ the sound dolphins make

3 What was Annie doing at the beginning of the story?

   ○ Feeding the fish

   ○ Sitting in the first row

   ○ Getting out of bed

   ○ Talking to the dolphin trainer

4 Which of these tells something that is make-believe?

   ○ Annie touched the dolphin's nose.

   ○ The dolphins jumped in the air.

   ○ The dolphins spoke English.

   ○ The workers carried buckets of fish.

Directions: Read the story. Then read each question about the story. Choose the best answer to the question. Mark the space for the answer you have chosen.

Alice Asks for Help

Alice was a little girl who was very <u>independent</u>. She always liked to do things by herself. She never asked anyone for help.

One day while walking home from school, Alice passed by her friend Pam's house. Pam and Pam's father were in the front yard of their house. They were surrounded by tools and pieces of wood. They were building a tree house.

"Wow, what a neat idea," thought Alice. "I think I'll build a tree house, too."

Alice went into her garage and gathered some wood, some nails, and a big bottle of glue.

Soon Alice's father came outside and saw her working. "Would you like some help, Alice?" he asked.

"No, thanks. I can <u>manage</u> it by myself," said Alice, and she continued working.

Alice worked for two days to make the four walls of the tree house. But when she tried to put the walls together, they were crooked and they wouldn't stay together. The house fell apart.

Alice was very upset. Just then, her father walked outside. He saw the pieces of the house on the grass. "This isn't so bad!" he said. "You've done very well by yourself. This will be easy to finish."

"Really?" Alice asked. "Can you give me some help, please?"

"Sure," her father said. He helped her fix the walls. Working together, they finished the tree house in just a few hours.

That afternoon, Alice invited her friends over to play in the new tree house. She invited her father to come up, too.

"You know what, Dad? I realized today that sometimes it's okay to ask for help," Alice said with a smile.

1 The main idea of this story is that Alice —

   O builds a tree house

   O learns that it's okay to ask for help

   O wants to play with her friends

   O worked for two days

2 How does Alice feel about her father's help at the end of the story?

   O Calm

   O Afraid

   O Pleased

   O Unhappy

3 In this story, an independent person is someone who —

   O uses tools

   O likes to be quiet

   O wants a lot of help

   O does things without help

4 Which is a FACT in this story?

   O Alice gathered wood and nails.

   O Alice had more friends than Pam.

   O Pam was building a dog house.

   O Alice's dad was on vacation.

5 The word manage in this story means —

   O play

   O do

   O saw

   O explain

6 What is this story mostly about?

   O Pam and Pam's dad built a tree house for Pam and Alice to share.

   O Alice put the tree house walls together but they were all crooked.

   O Alice invited her friends and her father over to play in her new tree house.

   O Alice tries to build a tree house by herself, but needs help in the end.

7 How did Alice feel when the walls she put together fell apart?

   O Upset

   O Confused

   O Joyful

   O Curious

Name: _____   **Date:** _____

Directions: Read the story. Then read each question about the story. Choose the best answer to the question. Mark the space for the answer you have chosen.

July 12

Dear Mom,

I'm having a great time here at summer camp. The food isn't very good. But there are lots of things to do. Monday we went out on the lake in canoes. I even tried riding a horse!

Something scary happened to me yesterday. The whole camp went on a field trip to see a cheese factory. It was really interesting to see how they make cheese. I never saw so much cheese in all of my life!

At 3:00 the bus was supposed to leave to go back to the camp. I was so <u>fascinated</u> by the factory that I forgot to look at the clock. It was after 3:30 by the time I realized that I was late.

I was worried. I looked around, but didn't see anyone from our camp. I wasn't sure what to do. So I went back to the front desk to ask for help. I told the woman behind the desk that I was lost.

"Are you from the summer camp?" she asked.

"Yes," I said.

"Your friends are waiting for you outside in the bus," she replied. And she showed me where they were. Just then, one of the counselors came out of the factory. She had been looking everywhere for me.

My counselors on the bus were a bit worried that I was upset. When I told them that I was a little scared that they had left, they told me that they would never leave until everyone from camp is back on the bus. And my friends didn't mind waiting for me. While they were waiting, guess what they were doing. Eating cheese!

Love,

Paul

1 The word <u>fascinated</u> in this story means —

○ mistaken

○ careless

○ interested

○ bored

2 This story is mostly about —

○ Paul's trip to the factory

○ Paul eating some cheese

○ the food at camp

○ Paul calling his mother

3 Paul forgot to look at the —

○ bus

○ factory

○ camp

○ clock

4 How did Paul feel when he realized he was late?

○ Annoyed

○ Sorry

○ Happy

○ Worried

Name: _____ Date: _____

Directions: Read the story. Then read each question about the story. Choose the best answer to the question. Mark the space for the answer you have chosen.

Doctors

"Oh, my! I don't feel well. I'd better see a doctor!" Everyone is very glad that there are doctors. They help us to get better when we are sick or hurt. They are some of the most important people in town. Their job is to keep people healthy and strong!

There are doctors for every part of the human body. Some doctors take care of your whole body. Other doctors work only on your bones and teeth. Other doctors know about ears, eyes, noses, and throats. There are also special doctors that work only on brains or hearts.

Sometimes people go to a doctor even when they are not sick. This kind of visit is called a <u>check-up</u>. Doctors like to check up on children because children grow quickly. Doctors want to make sure that the children are growing properly.

People become doctors for many reasons. Some want to help people. Others want to learn about what keeps people healthy. Some are scientists who look for cures to diseases. A person must be very smart to become a doctor.

It takes many years of school before a doctor has <u>patients</u>. Before a doctor treats people, he or she must know a lot. By the time he or she has patients, the doctor knows how to find out what is wrong with someone. He or she knows how to take care of the problem. Whether a person has a broken bone or needs some medicine for a cold, the doctor is always there to help!

1 The story says that people think that doctors —

    ○ should wear different clothes

    ○ only take care of old people

    ○ are always sick

    ○ are always there to help

2 This story is mostly about —

    ○ tools doctors use to look in a person's throat

    ○ the kinds of work doctors do

    ○ the kinds of medicine people need

    ○ getting better after a bad cold

3 In this story, a <u>check-up</u> is —

    ○ a visit to the doctor when the person is not sick

    ○ a place where doctors go to school

    ○ a broken bone

    ○ medicine for a cold that you get when you're on vacation

4 In this story, which of these is **NOT** a fact about doctors?

    ○ A doctor's job is to keep people healthy and strong.

    ○ A person doesn't have to be very smart to become a doctor.

    ○ Sometimes people go to a doctor even when they are not sick.

    ○ There are special doctors that work only on hearts.

5 In this story, <u>patients</u> are people who —

    ○ go out for ice cream

    ○ visit the doctor

    ○ play soccer

    ○ make dinner

6 It is important for doctors to go to school so that —

    ○ they can learn about trees

    ○ there will be fewer ambulances

    ○ they can help people

    ○ they can read magazines

Directions: Read the story. Then read each question about the story. Choose the best answer to the question. Mark the space for the answer you have chosen.

The Book Fair

The school book sale was held during the first week of November, and Vikken loved to read. In fact, there was nothing in the world that Vikken enjoyed more than to read new and exciting books.

The day before the book sale, Mrs. Danforth gave each of her students an order sheet. The sheet showed the rules for shopping at the book fair. "Make sure that you get your parents to sign at the bottom," Mrs. Danforth said. "Otherwise we can't let you buy any books." Vikken rushed right home after school and had his mother sign his order sheet.

ANNUAL BOOK FAIR ORDER SHEET   Location: Cafeteria
                                      Wednesday, November 4th

Student's Name _____   6:00 P.M.– 8:00 P.M.

Teacher's Name _____

RULES—

Students must have their parents sign the bottom of this form. Parents should also note the amount of money that students are allowed to spend.

All book sales are final.

Books will be arranged in <u>sections</u>: Mystery, Fairy Tales, Biography, Sports, and Adventure.

Use this sheet as your receipt.

BOOK   COST   QUANTITY   SUBTOTAL

_____

_____

_____

PARENT'S SIGNATURE _____   TOTAL _____

---

1 How did Vikken feel when he heard about the book fair?

   ○ Excited

   ○ Calm

   ○ Sad

   ○ Bored

2 Which type of books will **NOT** be sold at the fair?

   ○ Mystery

   ○ Sports

   ○ Travel

   ○ Biography

3 The word <u>sections</u> in this story means —

   ○ groups

   ○ books

   ○ rules

   ○ chapters

4 What time will the Book Fair end?

   ○ 6:00 P.M.

   ○ 7:00 P.M.

   ○ 8:00 P.M.

   ○ 9:00 P.M.

5 This story is mostly about how Vikken —

   ○ chose magazines at the fair

   ○ learned more about the book fair

   ○ asked his mother to come to the fair

   ○ had his mother sign his order sheet

Name: _____ Date: _____

Directions: Read the story. Then read each question about the story. Choose the best answer to the question. Mark the space for the answer you have chosen.

Cindy's New Bicycle

Cindy and her mother were on their way to the supermarket. They were going to buy some food for dinner. As they arrived at the store, they noticed a sign that read "Huge Garage Sale Today."

Cindy's mother knew that Cindy wanted a bicycle. She thought that this would be a good day to buy one. "Let's go see if they have any bicycles," she suggested, and Cindy agreed.

They left the supermarket and followed the directions on the sign. They walked down the street and around the corner. At the end of the block they saw a big red house with a white fence. Next to the house was a yard full of things for sale.

A red bike caught Cindy's attention right away. She ran over to get a closer look. "How about this one, mom?" she asked.

Cindy's mother reminded her to take her time. "Make sure you find a bike that is the <u>proper</u> size for you," her mother said. "If it's too big to ride, it won't be any fun."

Cindy tried sitting on the red bike, but it was a little bit too big. She then tried a blue one, but it was a little bit too small. She looked at a few others, but she didn't see anything she liked.

"How about this one, Cindy?" her mother called from behind the house. Cindy followed her mother's voice to the backyard. There she saw her mother holding the most beautiful yellow bike. It was just the right size. Cindy couldn't wait to ride it home.

McGraw-Hill School Division

1 Where does this story mostly take place?

    ○ The supermarket

    ○ The school

    ○ The Garage Sale

    ○ Cindy's house

2 Which is a FACT in the story?

    ○ Cindy's favorite color is yellow.

    ○ Cindy bought a red bike.

    ○ Cindy's mom found a yellow bike.

    ○ Cindy has too many bikes.

3 Why did Cindy choose the yellow bike?

    ○ It was too big for her.

    ○ It was just the right size.

    ○ It was too small for her.

    ○ It was a boy's bike.

4 How did Cindy feel when she saw the yellow bike?

    ○ Unhappy

    ○ Dull

    ○ Thrilled

    ○ Puzzled

5 In this story the word <u>proper</u> means —

    ○ correct

    ○ biggest

    ○ equal

    ○ smallest

6 Where did Cindy's mom find the yellow bike?

    ○ In the backyard

    ○ Leaning on a tree

    ○ At the market

    ○ In her garage

Directions: Read the story. Then read each question about the story. Choose the best answer to the question. Mark the space for the answer you have chosen.

What happened to the seeds?

Marty went to his father one day and asked him how seeds grow. "Does a seed just know when to start growing? Do we have to help them?" Marty asked.

Marty's father suggested that they find out together. He asked Marty to find a clear plastic bag, a few seeds from his mother's garden, some paper towels, and a cup of water. "I remember an experiment that I tried when I was your age," Marty's father said. "Let's see if it can help us understand how seeds grow."

Marty returned with all the items, and he and his father set to work. First they soaked the paper towels in the water from the cup. Then they folded the wet towels into thick squares and tucked them inside the plastic bag. They took the handful of seeds that Marty had gotten from his mother and laid them inside the bags on the towels. The towels were like small beds for the seeds. Marty's father loosely folded the bags and hung them on a window in the kitchen where they would get plenty of sunlight.

"Now what?" asked Marty.

"Now we wait. Many things that happen in nature can only be seen if you're patient. All things take time," Marty's father said.

So they waited. Each day Marty would check the bag to see if anything new had happened. Day after day, nothing changed.

One day, a few weeks after they began the experiment, Marty forgot to check the seeds before he went to school. He ran home, hoping he hadn't missed anything exciting. To his shock, the seeds had begun to sprout tiny <u>shoots</u>! The shoots were green and were growing up toward the sun. They looked like baby leaves. The roots were growing down and looked white and fragile. Marty called his father over and excitedly showed him what was happening.

"That's how seeds grow, Marty," his father said. "They need air, water, and sunlight. They're very delicate when they're young, like all things in nature. But they'll do just fine if you give them a little time."

1 How did Marty feel when the seeds began to grow?

○ Disappointed

○ Cheerful

○ Angry

○ Fearful

2 Which of these happened last in the story?

○ Marty asked how seeds grow.

○ Marty forgot to check the seeds.

○ Marty's father hung the bags in the window.

○ Marty got seeds from his mother's garden.

3 Marty and his father placed the seeds in the bag because —

○ they were doing an experiment

○ they needed a place to store them

○ there was no place to plant them

○ the seeds were old

4 What is the main idea of this story?

○ Marty finds a use for a plastic bag.

○ Marty asked his father how seeds grow.

○ Marty learns how seeds grow.

○ Marty's father helps him with his homework.

5 Which is a FACT from the story?

○ Seeds need air to grow.

○ Plants only need sunshine to live.

○ Plants can grow to be six feet tall.

○ Marty's father was excited.

6 The word <u>shoots</u> in this story means —

○ new plant growth

○ a tree branch

○ seeds that are dead

○ a new place in the ground

Directions: Read the story. Then read each question about the story. Choose the best answer to the question. Mark the space for the answer you have chosen.

Ginny was proud when the play she was in won the Third Grade Contest. The play was about a family of chipmunks who lived in a pine forest. All of the students worked very hard to learn their parts. Ginny wanted to keep a scrapbook of all of the plays she was going to be in. Her mother took some pictures, and she saved the program from the play.

The Third Grade Class of Hamilton Elementary School
presents
Chad and the Chipmunks in the Pine Forest
Friday, May 13, at 7:00 p.m. in the Lunch Room
Cookies and punch will be served from 6:00 p.m. to 7:00 p.m.
Description of the play:
"Chad and the Chipmunks in the Pine Forest" takes place
in a giant forest. Chad, a little chipmunk, is
very surprised to learn what happened
while he was sleeping.
CAST
(in the order they appear)
Chad Chipmunk..........Tomás Ruiz
Chipper Chipmunk..........Ginny Peterson
Mrs. Chipmunk..........Betsy Schmidt
Mr. Chipmunk..........Justin Washington
The Pine Tree..........Ashley Lu
The Pine Cone..........Kellie Goldman

Other Forest Animals: Juanita Hayes, Mark Farris,
Tammy Newman, Teresa Infante,
and Vincent Amario

The actors in the play would like to thank Mrs. Nuñez
for the chipmunk costumes, Mr. Carlson for the music,
Mr. Garshawn for the cookies and punch, and
Mr. Steinberg for building the chipmunk house.
ENJOY THE SHOW!

1 The word <u>cast</u> in this
   story means —

   ○ the people in the play

   ○ the time the play starts

   ○ the place where the play
      is held

   ○ the title of the play

2 Which is a FACT in this story?

   ○ Vincent Amario played
      Chipper Chipmunk.

   ○ Kellie Goldman played The
      Pine Cone.

   ○ Mrs. Nuñez made the
      cookies.

   ○ Mr. Steinberg played The
      Pine Tree.

3 Mrs. Chipmunk is —

   ○ a teacher at Hamilton
      Elementary School

   ○ a character in the play

   ○ Ginny's mother

   ○ the gym teacher

4 According to the program, what
   will happen before the play
   begins?

   ○ Everyone will go home.

   ○ The lights will be turned on.

   ○ Cookies and punch will
      be served.

   ○ The stage will be taken down.

5 Juanita Hayes helped with the
   play by —

   ○ playing a forest animal

   ○ baking cookies

   ○ playing Chad Chipmunk

   ○ making posters

Name: _____ Date: _____

Directions: Read the story. Then read each question about the story. Choose the best answer to the question. Mark the space for the answer you have chosen.

Chess

Chess is one of the oldest games in the world. It was first played over 2,000 years ago in India. Today it is played all over the world.

The chessboard is just like the board used for checkers. It has 32 black squares and 32 white squares. At the beginning of the game, players put their pieces on the chessboard. Each player has sixteen pieces: one king, one queen, two bishops, two knights, two rooks, and eight pawns. One player uses white pieces, and the other player uses black pieces.

Each of the pieces can only move in certain ways. The pawns, for example, can only move forward. The other pieces can move forward and backward. When you first start to play, it takes a few hours to learn the ways that all the pieces can move. To make it easier to tell the pieces apart, each of these pieces has a different shape. For example, the knights are <u>typically</u> shaped like horses, and the rooks are usually shaped like castles.

The players take turns moving their pieces on the board. Each player tries to <u>capture</u> the pieces of the other player. The game is over when one player takes the other player's king.

Every few years there is a chess contest for the best players in the world. When they play, a game of chess can take a very long time. Sometimes a single game lasts for hours.

Even without a partner, you can still play chess. Today there are computers that play chess just as well as people can!

1 In this story, the word <u>typically</u> means —

   ○ differently

   ○ sadly

   ○ softly

   ○ usually

2 The word <u>capture</u> in this story means —

   ○ take

   ○ hit

   ○ swing

   ○ call

3 Chess is played —

   ○ by adults only

   ○ in Texas only

   ○ all over the world

   ○ by teachers only

4 In order for people to be able to tell the chess pieces apart, the pieces are —

   ○ shaped like horses

   ○ all the same

   ○ spotted and striped

   ○ shaped differently

5 This story is mostly about —

   ○ how chess is played

   ○ what chess players eat

   ○ when chess pieces are moved

   ○ where chess is played

Name: _____ **Date:** _____

Directions: Read the story. Then read each question about the story. Choose the best answer to the question. Mark the space for the answer you have chosen.

Weathering the Storm

Deirdre and her cousin Max spent some time with their Aunt Jenna at her house by the ocean. Deirdre kept a record in her diary of the things they did. Here are some of the entries she made.

August 15th

I love the smell of salt water that is in the air. And I love the fact that the sound of the ocean follows me wherever I go. It's like a soft whisper in the background all the time. It's nice to fall asleep and to wake up to the sound of the waves rolling in. Today Aunt Jenna and I walked on the beach and watched seagulls. Aunt Jenna is really lucky to live here. She says that she spends almost an hour every day doing nothing but sitting back and watching the water. She has a big back porch that faces the ocean. We sit on it when we're not swimming or playing in the sand. This is one of the best places to visit.

August 16th

There was a really big storm today. The ocean looked totally different during the storm. It can be very frightening! The sky was as dark as night and lightning leapt from the clouds! The thunder went BOOM! BOOM! BOOM! <u>Immense</u> waves crashed on the beach. I had to cover my ears a few times. I'm glad I was not on a ship out on the sea today! I wonder how the sailors in the olden days would have handled those huge waves. Aunt Jenna says that part of living by the ocean is learning about the water. Sometimes it can be lots of fun. But sometimes it can be dangerous.

August 17th

Everything was calm today. It's as if there was never a storm. The only clue was the shells and driftwood that had washed up on shore. Max and I played in the water for a long time. Max showed me how to body surf. The waves rolled in and we jumped into them and let them carry us back to the beach. It was great fun!

1 The word <u>immense</u> in this diary means —

   ○ tricky

   ○ huge

   ○ brave

   ○ calm

2 What is the main idea of the diary?

   ○ The friendship of Deirdre and her cousin Max

   ○ A visit to the beach

   ○ A bird watching trip

   ○ An old California town

3 Where is the diary being written?

   ○ At Max's house

   ○ On a boat

   ○ In California

   ○ At Aunt Jenna's house

4 Which of these happened on August 17th?

   ○ Playing in the water

   ○ Walking on the beach

   ○ Listening to thunder

   ○ Watching seagulls

Directions: Read the story. Then read each question about the story. Choose the best answer to the question. Mark the space for the answer you have chosen.

Sal and the Shooting Star

Last summer, Sal's family went on vacation. They stayed in a cottage in the country. One night after dinner, Sal was out on the porch with his father. The sky was very clear. Sal could see millions of stars in the sky. He had never seen so many stars in all his life. Suddenly, one of the stars seemed to fall out of the sky!

"Did you see that?" his Dad asked.

"Yes, what was it?" said Sal.

"It was a shooting star. Shooting stars streak across the sky and leave a bright tail behind them. They are gone as quickly as they appear. It's supposed to be good luck to see one. Should we make a wish?" his father asked.

Sal made a wish. Then he said, "Where did it go, Dad? Can all the stars fall out of the sky?" Sal tried to imagine what the sky would look like without all those stars in it.

"No," Sal's Dad said. "Stars don't really fall out of the sky. In fact, the stars that shoot across the sky aren't really stars at all."

"What are they?" Sal asked.

"They're called <u>meteors</u>," said Sal's Dad. "They're pieces of rock that were floating through space. The earth's gravity pulls them in out of space as we pass by them."

"If it's a rock," said Sal, "why does it look like a star?"

"It's going very fast," said Sal's dad. "So fast that when it enters the air around the Earth, it starts to burn up. Most meteors burn up when they are high up in the sky. Even a meteor the size of a car will usually burn up entirely before it hits the ground."

"Are the meteors dangerous when they hit the ground?" asked Sal.

"They could be. But there is very little chance that the meteor will even get that far. I wouldn't worry about that," his father replied.

"Sometime I'd like to find a meteor that has hit the earth," said Sal.

"Well, keep looking," said Sal's Dad. "And maybe someday you'll find one."

1 The word <u>meteors</u> in this story means —

   ○ groups of planets

   ○ air around Earth

   ○ the sun

   ○ pieces of rock

2 This story is mostly about —

   ○ a man who teaches science class

   ○ a boy who is learning about shooting stars

   ○ a boy who makes a wish

   ○ people that disappear

3 What was Sal doing at the beginning of the story?

   ○ Talking to his father

   ○ Getting ready for school

   ○ Staying at a friend's cottage

   ○ Fishing with his mother

4 Which of these tells something that is make-believe?

   ○ A meteor the size of a car will usually burn up entirely before it hits the ground.

   ○ One night Sal was out on the porch with his father.

   ○ All of the stars will burn out and fall out of the sky.

   ○ Shooting stars are gone as quickly as they appear.

Directions: Read the story. Then read each question about the story. Choose the best answer to the question. Mark the space for the answer you have chosen.

David Stillwell couldn't wait for evening to arrive. The school band was giving its last concert of the year. David and his friends had been practicing for weeks to get ready for the show.

David's parents came home from work and they ate dinner quickly. Then they all <u>headed</u> to the school gym. When they arrived, they found one of David's classmates standing at the door. She gave them each a program that described the concert.

Jackson School Band
Spring Concert

Saturday, May 25
7:00 p.m.
Billings Auditorium

Program
Twinkle Twinkle Little Star
Three Blind Mice
Ring Around the Rosie
Hickory Dickory Dock

Musicians
(in alphabetical order)

Mark Andrews–Trombone   Tanya Oh–Cello
Kim Martin–Flute   David Stillwell–Trumpet
Julia Martinez–Clarinet   Kiaru Watanabe–Oboe
Ken Ng–Drums

Principal of Jackson School: Ms. Carey
Conductor: Mr. Simpson

Instruments will be shown in the
lobby before the concert.

1 How did David feel about the concert?

○ Upset

○ Confused

○ Excited

○ Curious

2 The word <u>headed</u> in this story means —

○ dropped

○ topped

○ stopped

○ went

3 What will happen before the concert begins?

○ The instruments will be put away.

○ The band will play *Ring Around the Rosie.*

○ The instruments will be shown.

○ Everyone will go home.

4 Ken Ng helped with the concert by —

○ playing the trombone

○ handing out programs

○ playing the drums

○ helping the principal

5 Ms. Carey is —

○ the conductor

○ a musician

○ the music teacher

○ the principal

6 Which is a FACT in this story?

○ David Stillwell played the trumpet.

○ Tanya Oh played the flute.

○ The concert was held on Friday.

○ Julia Martinez enjoyed playing in the concert.

Name: _____ **Date:** _____

Directions: Read the story. Then read each question about the story. Choose the best answer to the question. Mark the space for the answer you have chosen.

Eddie Learns to Cook

Eddie woke up on a sunny Sunday in June. Every Sunday, Eddie's father made pancakes for breakfast for Eddie, his grandmother, and his Uncle Gerry. Eddie was hungry, so he jumped out of bed and ran downstairs to the kitchen. His father was already busy. The flour and milk were on the counter, and he was preparing to make pancakes.

"Can I help?" Eddie asked.

"Sure," his father replied. "Why don't you take four eggs out of the refrigerator? Then you can crack them into a bowl and beat them."

Eddie found the egg carton in the back of the refrigerator. He picked out four large eggs and set them down next to the flour.

He had seen how his father cracked the egg against the counter, and then poured the egg into a bowl. Trying to imitate his father, Eddie took one of the eggs and hit it against the counter. The egg splattered all over both of them. "This is harder than it looks," he thought.

His father chuckled. "May I help you with that?" he asked.

"I think that's a good idea," said Eddie.

Eddie's father showed him how to gently tap an egg, just enough to break the shell. Eddie cracked the rest of the eggs himself and then began to beat them. Eddie even got to make some of the pancakes himself.

"Before you know it, you'll be a terrific chef," his father told him.

1 Who asked Eddie to take out the eggs?

   ○ Eddie's mother

   ○ Grandmother

   ○ Uncle Gerry

   ○ Eddie's father

2 Which of these happened last in this story?

   ○ Eddie woke up in the morning.

   ○ Eddie gathered eggs from the refrigerator.

   ○ Eddie cracked eggs open the right way.

   ○ Eddie ran downstairs.

3 Eddie's father chuckled because —

   ○ he likes making pancakes

   ○ egg splattered on him

   ○ Grandmother was coming to breakfast

   ○ Eddie was hungry

4 Next Sunday, Eddie will probably want to —

   ○ sleep in late

   ○ go somewhere else for pancakes

   ○ eat cereal

   ○ crack all the eggs

5 At the beginning of the story, how did Eddie feel?

   ○ Sleepy

   ○ Hungry

   ○ Excited

   ○ Silly

6 In this story, which of these is a FACT?

   ○ There are many cartons of eggs in the refrigerator.

   ○ Eddie wants to help his father make pancakes.

   ○ Grandmother showed him how to gently tap an egg.

   ○ The flour and the milk were in the cupboard.

Directions: Read the story. Then read each question about the story. Choose the best answer to the question. Mark the space for the answer you have chosen.

Mama Bird Sings a Pretty Song

Three little eggs hatched in a nest one day. The nest was high up in a tree. The mama bird looked at her baby birds with pride. She had been waiting for them to hatch for a long time!

"Good morning, little ones," she said to her babies. "How about some breakfast?"

The yellow baby bird opened his beak but could only say, "Cheep."

The red baby bird opened her beak but could only say, "Peep."

Mama bird was worried. "My, my," said the mama bird. "Why can't you speak?"

Just then, the blue baby bird opened its beak and said, "I'm very hungry and breakfast sounds like a very good idea. What is there to eat?"

"Well, I'm glad that at least one of you can speak," said the mama bird to her chick. "Let me go see what I can find for you. I'll be right back!" she said as she flew out of the nest.

"Peep," said the red baby bird.

"Cheep," said the yellow baby bird.

"I'm hungry," said the blue baby bird. "What's for breakfast?"

Soon the mama bird was back and had plenty of food for all of the birds in the nest. She couldn't figure out why two of her birds couldn't speak. She thought about it for a long time. Then she asked her neighbor, Mrs. Wren. Her neighbor said that it's <u>common</u> for baby birds not to speak for a few days.

The mama bird decided she would wait to see if her babies would all be speaking soon. She decided she would take them to the doctor at the end of the week if they were still peeping and cheeping. The next day, all of the baby birds woke up early.

"Good morning, mama," said the yellow baby bird.

"Good morning, mama," said the red baby bird.

"I'm hungry," said the blue baby bird.

"I'm <u>delighted</u>," said the smiling mama bird. "You can all speak! Some things are worth waiting for." She flew out of her nest to get some food for her babies. As she flew, she sang a pretty song.

1 The main idea of this story is that the baby birds —

○ are always singing pretty songs

○ learn to speak when they are ready

○ like to gather worms

○ learn to fly

2 The word <u>common</u> in this story means —

○ hidden

○ usual

○ confusing

○ strange

3 Which is a FACT in the story?

○ Mama bird couldn't figure out why two of her birds couldn't speak.

○ One baby bird was smarter than the other baby bird.

○ All the baby birds learned to speak at the same time.

○ The nest was on the porch.

4 How did the mama bird feel when two of the baby birds could only say, "Cheep"?

○ Angry

○ Worried

○ Joyful

○ Amused

5 In this story, the word <u>delighted</u> means —

○ happy

○ confused

○ curious

○ silly

6 Which is the first baby bird to say "Good morning" to the mama bird?

○ The yellow baby bird

○ The blue baby bird

○ The red baby bird

○ Mrs. Wren

7 What is this story mostly about?

○ Mama bird had to wait until the baby birds were ready to speak.

○ The baby birds taught the mama bird how to say "Peep."

○ The blue baby bird was very hungry and wanted breakfast.

○ Mama bird came back with food for all of the baby birds in the nest.

Directions: Read the story. Then read each question about the story. Choose the best answer to the question. Mark the space for the answer you have chosen.

Rex Reads About the Parks

Rex is trying to decide which amusement park to visit. He loves riding roller coasters. He has flyers from two parks in his area. Each park looks like a lot of fun! Rex is looking at these two flyers.

LAVALAND! FOR THE HOTTEST TIME IN TOWN!

Come to LavaLand to experience life on a volcano! Our volcano erupts every hour. You can watch lava pour out of the mountaintop.

In addition, you can take a ride inside our <u>artificial</u> volcano. It is made out of recycled materials, but it looks just like a real volcano. You will see what a volcano looks like inside and out.

There is fun here for everyone:

- rides
- tours
- games

There is always a lot of excitement in LavaLand! You'll want to come to LavaLand to see for yourself!!

COASTER CANYON—

THE PLACE TO GO IF YOU LOVE ROLLER COASTERS!

You've never seen anything quite like Coaster Canyon! Our amusement park has thirty roller coasters. We have roller coasters that are made entirely of wood and roller coasters that run on solar power. We have roller coasters that go underwater and ones that go underground. Have you ever been on a roller coaster that goes upside-down?

Here are some of our latest rides:

- The Underwater Coaster
- The Old-Fashioned Coaster
- The Tree-Top Coaster

We have the greatest roller coasters at Coaster Canyon!

---

1 In the LAVALAND ad, <u>artificial</u> means —

○ not real

○ large

○ fast

○ strange

2 What is Rex trying to decide?

○ Where to go on vacation

○ Which amusement park to visit

○ Which park has roller coasters

○ Where to see a volcano

3 Which of these is an OPINION in the advertisements that Rex read?

○ You'll want to come to LavaLand!

○ You can experience life on a volcano.

○ Coaster Canyon has roller coasters that run on solar power.

○ You can watch lava pour out of a mountaintop.

4 Why would Rex like Coaster Canyon?

○ He thinks the Underwater Coaster is fun.

○ He enjoys riding roller coasters.

○ He collects volcano models.

○ He likes to watch volcanoes erupt.

Name: _____ **Date:** _____

Directions: Read the story. Then read each question about the story. Choose the best answer to the question. Mark the space for the answer you have chosen.

Will Stan get a new puppy?

It was almost closing time at the pet shop when the front door opened. Stan bounced into the shop while his father held the door.

"How may I help you?" the shop owner asked.

"I'd like to see your puppies," Stan said. The pet shop owner went over to the puppy cages and looked inside.

"This one is a beautiful puppy," the owner said. He pointed to a spotted puppy. The puppy wagged its tail and went, "Yip, yip, yip!" Stan shook his head.

The owner pointed to another pup. "How about this one?" he asked. "She is very cute." He held up a big gray puppy. She had floppy ears and big, brown eyes. Her paws looked too big for her legs, and her tail flipped back and forth. "This puppy is very <u>curious</u>. She wants to learn everything she can. She is always running around sniffing things," the pet shop owner added. Stan shook his head again.

He pointed to a little black dog sleeping in the last cage. "What about that little puppy? Is it for sale?" Stan asked.

The pet shop owner picked up the tiny puppy and held him in his hands. He was about the same size as Stan's guinea pig.

"This dog is a miniature poodle," the man said. "When this puppy is full grown, he will be about the same size as a fully grown cat. Would you like to hold him?"

Stan smiled. The owner carefully handed the small puppy to Stan.

"Wow!" Stan exclaimed. "He feels like a little ball of fluff," Stan said. "I like this puppy, Dad. He is the perfect size for our apartment. He's not too big, and he'll have plenty of room to run around!" Stan exclaimed.

"I think that you're right, son," his father agreed.

1 Where does this story mostly take place?

   ○ Stan's school

   ○ The pet shop

   ○ Stan's apartment

   ○ The grocery store

2 Which is a FACT in the story?

   ○ Stan has too many cats.

   ○ Stan ran around the pet shop with the puppies.

   ○ Stan has a guinea pig.

   ○ The spotted puppy is beautiful.

3 Why did Stan choose the smallest puppy?

   ○ He wanted a strong dog.

   ○ That was the only puppy in the shop.

   ○ That puppy was like his old dog.

   ○ That dog would fit in his apartment.

4 How did Stan feel when he held the little black dog?

   ○ Silly

   ○ Selfish

   ○ Excited

   ○ Bored

5 In the story the word curious means —

   ○ wants to learn

   ○ tries to play

   ○ needs to eat

   ○ likes to jump

6 Where did the pet shop owner keep the puppies?

   ○ In the puppy cages

   ○ In the back yard

   ○ At his house

   ○ In the attic

Name: _____ Date: _____

Directions: Read the story. Then read each question about the story. Choose the best answer to the question. Mark the space for the answer you have chosen.

The Riverbed

Mr. Quigley's class dressed up in old clothes. They put on boots so they could explore the riverbed outside of town. The river had dried up a long time ago. Now it was just an old river bottom that ran through the desert. But Mr. Quigley pointed out that the riverbed could tell us a lot about what the river used to be like.

Everyone climbed down the side of the riverbed to the flat, rocky bottom. Mr. Quigley brought a bag and a small shovel. He scraped away several layers of rock and dirt. He said that the dirt was actually hard clay. "See how each layer of clay is a different color?" he asked. "That's because each layer was made at a different time. Some were made during different times in the same year. Others were made hundreds of years apart. During one time, there might have been a lot of rain or a lot of sun. Skeletons of fish and snails have been left in the clay when the water has dried up during very hot times. You can find all sorts of fossils in these layers of clay if you look for them. Here's one!"

Mr. Quigley pulled up his shovel. He looked carefully at a tiny creature in one of the bits of clay. Everyone moved in close to see what it was. Mr. Quigley picked the fossil up off the shovel and brushed away the extra clay. Then he passed his <u>discovery</u> around.

"It's a little fish!" Sally said happily, holding the fossil. She could see the head of the fish and its bones in the clay. It looked almost like a rock.

"That's right, Sally," Mr. Quigley said. "The ground you're standing on used to be the bottom of a river. At one time, it was full of all sorts of fish and animals. They're all gone now, but we can still find the clues they've left behind. These clues let us know that they were here."

"I wonder what other things we might find," Sam said.

"The only way to find out for sure is to take a look," Mr. Quigley said. He handed each student a small shovel from his bag and said, "Take a shovel, spread out, and happy hunting!"

1 When the story says that Mr. Quigley passed his <u>discovery</u> around, it means he passed around —

- ○ what was in the water
- ○ his shovel
- ○ a bucket
- ○ what he found

2 What happened first?

- ○ Everyone climbed down the side of the riverbed.
- ○ Mr. Quigley handed each student a small shovel from his bag.
- ○ Mr. Quigley's class dressed up in old clothes.
- ○ Mr. Quigley showed everyone that the dirt was actually hard clay.

3 What will Sam probably do next?

- ○ Dig in the riverbed for skeletons
- ○ Camp in the riverbed
- ○ Look for wild animals
- ○ Write a letter to his grandmother

4 How did Sally feel when she saw the fish head and bones in the clay?

- ○ Excited
- ○ Lonely
- ○ Worried
- ○ Afraid

5 Which sentence tells something that is make-believe?

- ○ Mr. Quigley told the students about the riverbed.
- ○ A dragon appeared in the riverbed.
- ○ Sally thought looking for tiny creatures was fun.
- ○ Sam and Sally liked to go on school trips.

Directions: Read the story. Then read each question about the story. Choose the best answer to the question. Mark the space for the answer you have chosen.

Games at Summer Camp

The second week of summer camp was going to start on Monday. Jorge agreed to plan the games for the younger children. He was getting worried. It was Sunday morning and he still hadn't been able to think of any games for the children to play. He remembered the games he played when he was younger. They were fun, but they did not require teams or have any rules.

"What games did you play in camp?" Jorge asked his older sister.

"I used to play flag football," his sister Pam said.

Jorge liked that idea. His sister couldn't remember all of the rules of the game. Jorge thought about the last time that his class went to the library. They had learned all about the reference section in the library. Jorge knew that he could find "How to" books about sports in the reference section. He could also ask the librarian for help.

Jorge's mom took him to the library that afternoon. Jorge found the perfect book. It had very clear instructions and pictures. Jorge was relieved. He checked the book out of the library.

When Jorge got home he looked up the rules for flag football. He thought the children would like the game. He also picked out three other games that he thought the younger children would enjoy. He wrote down the rules for flag football and made some notes about the other games he chose. He thought about how he would form the teams. Then he gathered together all of the items he would need for the games.

Jorge smiled. He was ready for Monday.

1   Why did Jorge go to the library?

   ○ To read about summer camps

   ○ To learn the rules for flag football

   ○ To get a book for the camp leader

   ○ To find a story about a different country

2   After Jorge read the library book, what did he think about flag football?

   ○ No one would like the game.

   ○ The game would be too hard for the children to learn.

   ○ The children would like the game.

   ○ Playing the game would be silly.

3   Where did Jorge get the idea to play flag football?

   ○ From his sister

   ○ From the kids at camp

   ○ From a book

   ○ From his father

4   What was Jorge's problem at the beginning of this story?

   ○ Jorge did not know how to play with younger children.

   ○ Jorge could not think of any games to play as a team.

   ○ Jorge did not want to go to summer camp.

   ○ Jorge did not want to go to the library.

5   When did Jorge go to the library?

   ○ After dinner

   ○ On the first day of camp

   ○ After talking to Pam

   ○ On Monday morning

6   This story is mostly about —

   ○ Playing darts at summer camp

   ○ What Jorge does on Tuesday morning

   ○ Going on a class trip to the library

   ○ How Jorge plans the games for camp

7   How did Jorge feel when he was ready for Monday?

   ○ Pleased

   ○ Careless

   ○ Puzzled

   ○ Disappointed

8   In this story, the word <u>relieved</u> means —

   ○ feeling sleepy

   ○ being angry

   ○ being afraid

   ○ feeling better

Name: _____ **Date:** _____

Directions: Read the story. Then read each question about the story. Choose the best answer to the question. Mark the space for the answer you have chosen.

Samantha Reads the Paper

Samantha and her mother were sitting at the breakfast table. She was drinking her orange juice and eating some cereal. Her mother handed her a newspaper article she thought Samantha might enjoy. Samantha loved to read. She liked anything that had to do with animals.

YOUNG DOLPHIN FINDS FRIEND

A young dolphin washed up on the beach yesterday. The dolphin was injured yesterday morning when a boat in the bay hit it by accident. The dolphin swam away before the boaters could try to help it. Later, the dolphin swam into shore. That's where he met eight-year-old Tiffany Lopez.

Miss Lopez was at the beach with her family. When she spotted the dolphin, she and her mother rushed over to it. They thought that it might need medical attention. When they found that the dolphin was hurt, they called the local police. The police called the local aquarium. The doctors who work there knew exactly what to do to help the dolphin.

Within a few hours, the dolphin was doing fine. The doctors gave him some medicine. Then they moved him to a special tank built just for dolphins. He will stay there until he is better. One of the doctors who helped thinks it will be about a week until the dolphin can go back to the bay.

Everyone thanks Tiffany Lopez and her family for getting the dolphin the help that it needed.

---

1 In this story, the word <u>spotted</u> means —

   ○ helped

   ○ rescued

   ○ covered

   ○ saw

2 What did Tiffany Lopez and her family do after she found the dolphin on the beach?

   ○ They went swimming.

   ○ They called the police.

   ○ They put the dolphin back in the water.

   ○ They went to the aquarium.

3 Which of these is an OPINION from the story?

   ○ Samantha's mother thought she might enjoy the newspaper article.

   ○ The doctors gave the dolphin some medicine and moved him to a special tank.

   ○ Tiffany Lopez was at the beach with her family.

   ○ A young dolphin swam to the shore.

4 Why would Samantha's mother think she would like the story YOUNG DOLPHIN FINDS FRIEND?

   ○ Tiffany Lopez is Samantha's friend.

   ○ She likes reading about animals.

   ○ She collects newspaper stories.

   ○ She likes to draw pictures of dolphins.

Directions: Read the story. Then read each question about the story. Choose the best answer to the question. Mark the space for the answer you have chosen.

The Attic

Ben and his brother Greg were cleaning their attic one rainy summer afternoon. They were looking through some old boxes. The boxes were covered with lots of dust. Ben pulled out one box. He sat down to look through it. Greg watched over his shoulder.

The boxes were filled with black and white <u>photographs</u>. The pictures looked very old. The boys didn't recognize anyone in the pictures. They agreed, though, that everyone looked very familiar. They also agreed that the photographs were a great discovery. They gathered up all the old photos and went to see their mother.

Their mother was in her office. She was busy preparing a report for work. Ben and Greg laid out the pictures on her filing cabinet. "Mom, who are the people in these pictures?" Ben asked.

Their mother smiled and asked, "Where did you find those old things? Did you find them as you were cleaning the attic?"

Ben and Greg nodded and asked their mother to tell them about the pictures.

"These are pictures of your ancestors. They are family members from a long time ago. Some of these pictures are over seventy-five years old. This one is of your great-grandmother Elizabeth and your great-great Uncle Timothy. They grew up in Europe. They came to America when they were young. It was many years before I was born."

Greg and Ben were amazed! They never knew that their family had come from another country! As they all looked through the rest of the pictures, Ben and Greg's mom told them great stories about the family. They learned about where the family had lived for many years. They also learned about how their grandparents met one another. Hearing the stories made the boys feel closer to their family. Even though they would never meet the people in the pictures, they felt as if they knew them a little better.

1 Where were the pictures?

○ In the filing cabinet

○ In the garage

○ In the attic

○ Under the bed

2 How did Ben and Greg feel about finding the pictures?

○ Worried

○ Sad

○ Pleased

○ Tired

3 In this story, the word <u>photographs</u> means —

○ dust

○ books

○ clothes

○ pictures

4 When did Ben and Greg make their find?

○ In the winter

○ In the afternoon

○ At night

○ When it was raining

5 What will the boys probably do next?

○ Put the pictures away

○ Go outside and play

○ Make a snack

○ Watch television

6 Which of these is NOT a fact from the story?

○ The pictures were of family members from a long time ago.

○ Greg knew the names of everyone in the pictures.

○ Ben and Greg's mother was in her office preparing a report.

○ Ben and Greg were in their attic looking through some old boxes.

7 How did Ben and Greg feel when they learned their relatives came from another country?

○ Amazed

○ Foolish

○ Selfish

○ Confused

8 Which of these could have REALLY happened?

○ Ben and Greg found some pictures.

○ The attic walls spoke to Ben and Greg.

○ The pictures talked to Ben and Greg.

○ The pictures were as big as the house.

Directions: Read the story. Then read each question about the story. Choose the best answer to the question. Mark the space for the answer you have chosen.

The Car Race

Jake ran home from his Scout meeting as fast as he could. He couldn't wait to tell his father about the model race car contest that was coming up. As Jake was washing up before dinner, his father read the handout about the race.

Jake thought about what he would need to build his race car. He would have to find a small block of wood for the body. He'd also need some wheels and some oil to make the wheels spin faster.

Jake's father told him that each car had to weigh at least eight ounces. If the car was too light when they were finished, they could tape some coins on the bottom to make it heavier. Jake began to make a <u>sketch</u> in his notebook of how he wanted his car to look.

Scout Troop Annual Homemade Race Car Contest
November 27

RULES:
1. Every car must weigh at least 8 ounces.
2. Every car must be at least 4 inches long.
3. Contestants must put their name on their cars.
4. Contestants must check in with their cars by 9:00 A.M.

SCHEDULE:
First Round – 10:00 A.M.
Second Round – 10:30 A.M.
Third Round – 11:00 A.M.
Lunch - 12:00 NOON
Semifinals – 2:00 P.M.
Finals – 3:00 P.M.
Presentation of Awards – 3:30 P.M.

PRIZES:
Awards will be given for first place, second place, and third place.
There will be three special awards: one for the car that weighs closest to eight ounces, one for the car voted most beautiful, and one for the car voted funniest looking.

---

1 How did Jake feel when he told his father about the Homemade Race Car Contest?

   ○ Sad

   ○ Disappointed

   ○ Afraid

   ○ Eager

2 To enter his race car in the contest, Jake would need to —

   ○ build a car that weighs two ounces

   ○ put his name on his car

   ○ check in by 12:00 NOON

   ○ create a car that is three inches long

3 The word <u>sketch</u> in this story means —

   ○ a drawing

   ○ a photograph

   ○ a letter

   ○ an award

4 What time will the Semifinals begin?

   ○ 12:00 NOON

   ○ 2:00 P.M.

   ○ 3:00 P.M.

   ○ 3:30 P.M.

5 This story is mostly about how Jake —

   ○ built a model race car with his father

   ○ learned the facts about the race car contest

   ○ liked to enter contests and get prizes

   ○ added coins to his car for more weight

Directions: Read the story. Then read each question about the story. Choose the best answer to the question. Mark the space for the answer you have chosen.

What is funny about Victor's new job?

Victor wanted to make some extra money so that he could buy a new football. He asked his mother if she knew of anyone in the neighborhood who needed help with any chores.

"As a matter of fact, Mrs. Chinney told me that she's looking for a babysitter. That is a lot of responsibility. Are you prepared for it?" his mother asked. Victor promised his mother that he could do it. They called Mrs. Chinney, and she asked Victor to come over on Thursday night. Victor was very excited.

When Thursday night finally came, Mrs. Chinney invited Victor inside and introduced him to Thurman. Thurman was a 12-pound cat.

"I thought you needed a babysitter," Victor said nervously. He had never spent much time around cats. And Thurman was a very large cat!

"Thurman is my baby," Mrs. Chinney said. "You two will have fun together. I'll be back in a few hours." She turned and walked out the door.

For the next few hours, Victor tried to play with Thurman. He tossed a ball of yarn around because he'd heard that cats liked to play with string. Thurman did nothing. He tried to pet Thurman. Thurman hissed at him, and shot his tail straight up into the air. When Victor ignored the cat, Thurman climbed into his lap and cuddled. When Victor tried to feed Thurman, the cat just rolled over and went to sleep. But when Thurman tipped over a glass of milk, there he was, licking it up.

When Mrs. Chinney came home, Victor was miserable.

"How did everything go with my baby?" Mrs. Chinney asked.

"Oh, it was great," Victor said frowning.

"Really?" Mrs. Chinney asked. She looked concerned.

Victor was so upset that he had a tough time concealing it. "He does whatever he pleases," Victor moaned. "He goes where he wants, and he listens only when he cares to. He didn't do anything I wanted him to do, but he did everything I didn't want him to do. He's impossible!"

Mrs. Chinney only smiled. "Excellent!" she said. "You've learned your first and most important lesson about cats. We will see you next Thursday, then," she said. "I think you'll do just fine as Thurman's weekly sitter! How does that sound?"

1 Victor thought babysitting would be —

   ○ exciting

   ○ difficult

   ○ dull

   ○ tough

2 Victor told Mrs. Chinney that babysitting had been great because he didn't want to —

   ○ clean his room

   ○ play with his brothers

   ○ eat his vegetables

   ○ hurt Mrs. Chinney's feelings

3 After babysitting for Thurman, Victor will probably —

   ○ play with his friends

   ○ try to get a different job

   ○ get a cat of his own

   ○ go to the movies

4 This story is mostly about a boy who —

   ○ has a challenging job

   ○ does his homework

   ○ walks neighborhood dogs

   ○ likes to babysit

5 Which of these happened last?

   ○ Thurman hissed.

   ○ Victor put out food for Thurman and Thurman rolled over and went to sleep.

   ○ Victor wanted extra money.

   ○ Mrs. Chinney offers Victor the job of being Thurman's weekly babysitter.

Directions: Read the story. Then read each question about the story. Choose the best answer to the question. Mark the space for the answer you have chosen.

Mrs. Honeywell's Letter to Nicole

Nicole's next-door neighbor, Mrs. Honeywell, was on vacation. Nicole had agreed to take care of her house while she was gone. Every day she went over to Mrs. Honeywell's house for half an hour to do a few chores. Nicole was proud that Mrs. Honeywell trusted her so much.

The first time Nicole went to Mrs. Honeywell's house, she found a letter with instructions for everything she needed to do.

Nicole,

Thank you very much for agreeing to care for my house while I am away. You are a great help. Here are all of the things that need to be done.

Plants: There are three plants in the living room. Please water the tall one every day. The two shorter plants should be watered every other day. If any dead leaves fall on the floor, please pick them up and put them in the garbage.

Newspaper: I have asked the newspaper boy not to deliver the paper this week. If he forgets, and you find a newspaper in front of the house, please bring it inside.

Mail: Please <u>collect</u> the mail from my mailbox every day. Place it in a pile on the table in the living room.

Birds: The birds have enough food for the week. Please don't feed them. Open the water bottle every few days to see if there is enough water inside. If it looks like the birds need more water, please refill the bottle.

If you have any problems, call Mrs. Johnson. She lives across the street and is usually home during the day. In case of an emergency, she will know how to contact me.

I should be back in one week, but I might be able to stay for two weeks! I'll call you if I'll be staying longer.

Thank you again,

Mrs. Honeywell

1 The word <u>collect</u> in this story means —

○ find

○ share

○ gather

○ put

2 This story is mostly about —

○ chores

○ birds

○ trips

○ neighbors

3 According to the letter, Nicole does **NOT** have to —

○ bring in the newspaper

○ feed the birds

○ water the plants

○ pile the mail on the table

4 Mrs. Honeywell's letter shows that she is —

○ mean

○ angry

○ thoughtful

○ upset

5 In case of an emergency, Nicole should call —

○ her teacher

○ Mrs. Johnson

○ Mrs. Honeywell

○ the mailman

6 If Mrs. Honeywell stays on vacation for two weeks, Nicole will probably —

○ continue to do the chores

○ not go back to Mrs. Honeywell's house

○ forget to water the plants

○ join Mrs. Honeywell on her trip

7 At the beginning of the story, Nicole feels —

○ sleepy

○ sad

○ worried

○ proud

Directions: Read the story. Then read each question about the story. Choose the best answer to the question. Mark the space for the answer you have chosen.

A Different Saturday Afternoon

Ted didn't get a chance to see his friend Sam very often. They went to different schools. Ted lived on one side of town, and Sam lived on the other. They usually got together only on the weekends.

Ted was supposed to go visit Sam at two o'clock one Saturday afternoon. Earlier in the day, though, Sam called on the telephone. "I'm sorry, Ted. I have a homework assignment that I have to do before I can meet you. My teacher gave it to me yesterday. I think it's going to take me a long time. Can we meet next weekend instead?" Sam asked.

Ted was sad. He was looking forward to showing Sam the new toy he had just completed making. Ted planned to be an inventor when he grew up. He had worked hard on his new toy and wanted to share it. "That's too bad," he said to Sam. "Can you can come over after you've done your homework?" he asked.

"I already asked my mother and she said no. My parents are going out tonight and my cousin, Frank, is coming over to watch me," Sam replied.

Ted thought for a moment. He knew that a good inventor should also be good at solving problems. He thought about the problem he and Sam were having. Then he came up with the perfect solution!

"Sam, what kind of homework do you have to do?" Ted asked.

"It's my science homework. I have to finish a project and it's very hard," said Sam.

"I have an idea. If you would like, I can come over and help you with your homework," Ted said. "If it's okay with your parents, I'd like that. Then you and I can still see each other."

Sam thought that it was a great idea. He had Ted wait while he asked his parents. When he came back to the telephone, he sounded very happy. "You can come over, Ted. I hope you know something about how plants grow," Sam exclaimed.

"If I don't, I'm sure we can find the answer together," said Ted. "Let me go ask my mom to make sure that I can come over."

1 You can tell from this story that when you have <u>completed</u> something, you have —

○ started

○ played

○ finished

○ colored

2 The word <u>solution</u> in this story means —

○ solving something

○ building something

○ having a problem

○ doing homework

3 This story is mostly about —

○ Ted making a new toy

○ Sam going to Ted's house

○ changing plans for a Saturday afternoon

○ starting a geography project

4 Which sentence tells that something is make-believe?

○ Sam and Ted go to different schools.

○ Sam and Ted usually get together on the weekends.

○ Frank, Sam's cousin, was coming over to watch Sam.

○ The telephone said, "I have an idea."

Name: _____ Date: _____

Directions: Read the story. Then read each question about the story. Choose the best answer to the question. Mark the space for the answer you have chosen.

Why does a piano have so many notes?

Toji was excited because it was his first day of piano lessons. He knew that he had to learn a lot. There were so many notes. Toji wondered how people could play the notes so quickly.

Toji and his mother walked up the steps of an old house. His mother knocked on the door. The door creaked when it was opened by an old woman with gray hair.

"Hello! You must be Toji!" the woman said. "My name is Mrs. Mueller. Come in."

Toji and his mother went inside. It was a gigantic old house. Toji had never seen so many rooms. Each one was filled with large furniture, old pottery, and glass vases. The walls were covered with photographs. Then, they came to the last room in the house. Inside was nothing but a big, shiny black piano.

Toji looked at the piano. There were so many keys! The white ones went all the way from one side to the other. Sticking up in sets of two and three between the white keys were skinny black keys. Toji wondered how many keys there were. He started to count them. He had gotten about half way, when he accidentally pushed too hard on a key. It made a soft noise in the room.

Toji felt as if he had done something wrong, but Mrs. Mueller smiled at him. "There are lots of keys, aren't there?" she said.

Mrs. Mueller told Toji that there are 88 keys on the piano. "But," she said, "there are only eight different names for all of these notes." She explained that the piano starts with the note "C" on the left-hand side of the keyboard. After that, come the notes D, E, F, G, A, and B. The next note is "C" again. "The black keys are named a little differently," Mrs. Mueller said.

She put her left hand on the keys and played eight very low notes. After that, she reached out her right hand and played eight very high notes. Toji could hear how the higher set of notes was like the lower set.

"Now you try," said Mrs. Mueller.

Toji tried to play the notes like Mrs. Mueller had, but he twisted his fingers and made an awful noise.

"Just push one at a time. Start here." Mrs. Mueller showed Toji which key to push first.

Toji pushed the first key and then the second. He listened to each note. Toji knew that he was playing the same notes that Mrs. Mueller had played. When he played the eighth note, he knew he was finished. He turned around with a smile.

"Very good!" exclaimed Mrs. Mueller. "Soon you will be an expert pianist!"

1 The word <u>gigantic</u> in this
   story means —

   ○ large

   ○ tall

   ○ dusty

   ○ nice

2 This story is mostly about —

   ○ a boy who is learning to play
     the piano

   ○ the keys on a piano

   ○ how pianos are made

   ○ people that visit old houses

3 What was Toji doing at the
   beginning of the story?

   ○ Playing the notes

   ○ Saying the alphabet

   ○ Going to Mrs. Mueller's house

   ○ Looking at old pottery

4 Which of these tells something
   that is make-believe?

   ○ The black keys have different
     names than the white keys.

   ○ Mrs. Mueller played eight
     notes on the piano.

   ○ Toji jumped over Mrs.
     Mueller's house.

   ○ There are eighty-eight keys
     on the piano.

Name: _____   Date: _____

Directions: Read the story. Then read each question about the story. Choose the best answer to the question. Mark the space for the answer you have chosen.

What is challenging about Ravi's autumn chore?

Ravi wanted to help his mother with the autumn chores. He thought it would be fun. Ravi looked out at the front lawn. The orange leaves that had fallen from the trees were all over the ground. "Mom, I would like to help you by raking up all of the leaves on the ground," said Ravi.

"That would be a big help, Ravi," his mother said. She was very busy with all of the things she needed to do before winter came.

Ravi got a rake from the garage and started raking. He raked the leaves into piles. He would go back when all the leaves were in piles and rake them onto an old sheet. He could drag the leaves on the sheet off the edge of the lawn. That's where they always put their leaves. By next spring, there would be lots of good soil under the leaves. Ravi always looked there first when he needed worms for fishing.

When Ravi tried to rake the leaf piles onto the sheet, however, he found that it was not as easy as he thought it would be. Every time that he tried to rake the leaves onto the sheet, he ended up raking the sheet up, too. He tried and tried again, but he just couldn't do it. He went inside and asked his mother what he could do to keep the sheet in place as he raked the leaves.

"You can use an old metal bar that we have in the garage," his mother said. "If you lay it across the edge of the sheet where you are raking the leaves, it will hold the sheet in place. I'll come show you what I mean so that I can help if you would like me to."

Ravi and his mother began to rake together. His mother's idea worked. The metal bar was heavy enough to hold the sheet down while Ravi raked the leaves onto it. Soon, they had picked up every pile of leaves in the yard.

"We're done!" Ravi said with a sigh of relief. "That was a lot of hard work."

His mother smiled. "You did an excellent job, though. I appreciate your help."

Name: _____ **Date:** _____

1. Ravi had first thought that raking the yard would be —

   ○ fun

   ○ confusing

   ○ disappointing

   ○ amusing

2. Ravi could not get the leaves onto the sheet because —

   ○ the leaves were too heavy

   ○ he dropped the rake

   ○ the leaves kept blowing away

   ○ he kept raking up the sheet

3. Because of this experience, next time Ravi rakes the leaves he will probably try to —

   ○ go fishing with worms

   ○ use the metal bar from the beginning

   ○ stay inside the house

   ○ go sledding with his friends

4. This passage is mainly about a boy who —

   ○ sticks with a challenging job

   ○ gives up on raking the leaves

   ○ plays basketball with his friends

   ○ likes to play outside

5. Which of these happened last?

   ○ The orange leaves fell from the trees.

   ○ Ravi and his mother began to work together.

   ○ Ravi got a rake from the garage.

   ○ Ravi's mother told him how to keep the sheet in place.

Directions: Read the story. Then read each question about the story. Choose the best answer to the question. Mark the space for the answer you have chosen.

Kimberly's Trip to Grandma's House

When Kimberly opened her eyes, she wasn't sure where she was. It was cold, so she pulled the blankets up over her chin. She looked around at the strange room. Then she remembered. She had come with her aunt and uncle to Grandma's house in the country.

The floor was made of wood, and it was rough looking. It was very different from the carpet in her room at home. The curtains were not like her curtains in her room at home, either. They were much thicker. They made the room very dark. Kimberly heard people downstairs in the kitchen. She heard pots and pans banging and moving on the stove. She could smell breakfast cooking as she listened to the voices of her aunt, uncle, and grandma. Kimberly wasn't sure yet if she liked it here on the farm.

Kimberly was hungry, though, so she got out of bed. She saw that there were slippers waiting for her beside the bed. She slipped her feet into them. They were very big for her, but they were soft and furry on the inside. She was sure that they felt much nicer than the floor would feel.

Kimberly went over to the heavy curtains and pulled them open. She saw a barn and a field. There was a big brown cow in the field. On the other side of the field, she saw a forest. Off to the side of the barn, there was a pond. It was very quiet. All she heard outside were the birds and the farm animals. The sun was shining, and everything was green and bright.

Kimberly looked around the room. There were old pictures on the walls. She thought that she <u>recognized</u> the people in them. Suddenly Kimberly realized that the girls were her mother and her mother's two sisters! It made Kimberly feel strange to see a picture of her mother taken so long ago.

Kimberly got dressed and went downstairs.

"Hello!" said Uncle Mort as Kimberly came into the kitchen. "You're up early. Would you like some juice?"

"Yes, please," said Kimberly.

Kimberly's aunt came in with her Grandma from the next room. "Good morning," Aunt Maggie said. "We were just about to go out and collect the eggs from the chickens. Would you like to come along and help? After breakfast, we can go for a swim in the pond. How does that sound?"

"That sounds terrific!" said Kimberly. She took a sip of her juice. It sounded like there were going to be plenty of fun things to do here on the farm.

1 Before Kimberly saw the barn
   and the field, she —

   ○ took a sip of juice

   ○ saw a picture of her mother

   ○ talked to Uncle Mort

   ○ opened the curtains

2 What is the main idea of this
   story?

   ○ Kimberly ate breakfast with
     Uncle Mort.

   ○ Kimberly learns that visiting
     Grandma's house can be fun.

   ○ Kimberly saw a picture of her
     mother and her aunts.

   ○ Kimberly had fun at her Aunt
     Maggie's house.

3 In this story the word <u>recognized</u>
   means —

   ○ switched

   ○ liked

   ○ knew

   ○ met

4 When Kimberly first woke up,
   she felt —

   ○ happy

   ○ confused

   ○ amused

   ○ caring

5 After they collect eggs, Kimberly
   and Aunt Maggie will
   probably —

   ○ go for a bike ride

   ○ swim in the pond

   ○ make orange juice

   ○ clean the barn

Directions: Read the story. Then read each question about the story. Choose the best answer to the question. Mark the space for the answer you have chosen.

Leanne Finds the Best Way

Leanne didn't like tying her shoes. It took a long time, and it made her fingers hurt. Her fingers always got caught when she twisted and pulled the laces into bows.

"There must be a better way of doing this," Leanne thought to herself. One day Leanne decided she just wasn't going to tie her shoes at all.

"You'd better tie your shoes! You might trip and hurt yourself," Leanne's father said.

"No," Leanne answered, "I'm not tying my shoes anymore."

Leanne's father smiled and shook his head.

That day in school, Leanne was playing tag with her friends at recess. Tim was "it." He was running after Leanne, but Leanne wasn't worried. She knew she could run much faster than Tim could. Leanne waited until Tim had almost reached her, and then she turned and tried to <u>dash</u> away.

Oops! Leanne tripped over her shoelace and fell down on the grass. Her pants had bright green grass stains where her knees had hit the ground.

"There must be a better way of keeping these laces together," Leanne thought to herself as she stood up.

After recess, Leanne borrowed a stapler from her teacher and began stapling her shoelaces together.

"Why don't you just tie your shoes?" Leanne's teacher asked.

"I'm not doing that anymore," Leanne answered.

Leanne's teacher said nothing, but she smiled and shook her head.

After school, Leanne went over to her friend Megan's house to play video games. As Leanne and Megan were walking in the door, they heard Megan's mother in the kitchen. "Hi, girls, I've just finished washing the floors. Would you please take off your shoes?"

Leanne looked down at her shoes. Oops! Her laces were stapled together!

"I guess that wasn't a very good idea. There must be a better way of doing this," Leanne thought to herself as she <u>pried</u> the staples out of her shoes.

When it was time for Leanne to go home she looked down at her shoes. There were staples all around them on the floor. Her knee still hurt from where she fell on it during recess.

"Why don't you just tie your shoes?" asked Megan.

"You know," said Leanne, "I think that's the best way."

1 The main idea of this story is that Leanne —

○ talks to her teacher

○ learns from her own mistakes

○ likes to play video games

○ fell and hurt her knee

2 How did Leanne feel about tying her shoes at the end of the story?

○ Upset

○ Comfortable

○ Afraid

○ Sad

3 The word <u>dash</u> in this story means —

○ ride

○ run

○ skip

○ hide

4 Which is a FACT in the story?

○ Leanne stapled her shoelaces.

○ Leanne was taller than Megan.

○ Tim could run faster than Leanne.

○ Megan's mom drove Leanne home.

5 How did Leanne feel when Megan's mom asked her to take her shoes off?

○ Unhappy

○ Excited

○ Joyful

○ Amused

6 In this story, the word <u>pried</u> means —

○ pulled

○ tripped

○ played

○ stored

7 Who is the first person to tell Leanne to tie her shoes?

○ Megan

○ Tim

○ Her father

○ Her teacher

8 What is this story mostly about?

○ Leanne tried different ways to keep her laces together, but learned that tying them was the best way.

○ Leanne's father, Tim, and Megan showed Leanne how to tie her shoelaces.

○ Leanne asked her parents to buy her shoes without laces.

○ Leanne tripped on her shoelaces and got grass stains on her pants.

Directions: Read the story. Then read each question about the story. Choose the best answer to the question. Mark the space for the answer you have chosen.

Sasha's Boat Ride

Sasha was very unhappy. She got off the school bus with the rest of her class and stood in the parking lot. Her class had arrived at Pete's Pond. It was cloudy and cold. The bus ride had been too long, and now she felt a little sick.

The class went into the ranger station at the edge of the pond. A ranger named Bill Huff told them what kinds of animals they might see at the pond. Sasha wasn't listening. She liked to learn about animals, but she was too upset.

Then they all went out to the big boat. It was hard to get in. Sasha almost fell in the water. Sasha sat all of the way in the back of the boat. Ranger Bill stood at the other end of the boat. He was talking, but Sasha couldn't hear a word he said. The motor was too loud. Sasha was upset.

The boat started going down the river. Ranger Bill talked about the animals on the river. Sasha saw a turtle on a log. Nobody else saw it. The others were listening to Ranger Bill. Sasha didn't say anything about the turtle, but she felt a little better.

The river got narrower. There were trees on either side, and their branches hung over the river. Ranger Bill stood in the front of the boat and talked. The branches were very close to his big ranger hat. One branch was even lower than all the other branches were. POP! The low branch bumped into Ranger Bill's tall hat.

"What was that?" asked the ranger as his hat flew off his head. It landed in the water.

"My hat!" shouted Ranger Bill. He was concerned.

The boat was still going. It was going to leave the hat behind. Julie tried to grab the hat. She missed it. Then Maggie missed the hat, too. Tom tried to grab the hat. And he missed it. Felix couldn't even turn around fast enough to grab it.

They all missed the hat. Sasha was the last one in the boat. She was the last one to try to grab the hat.

Sasha reached out for the hat. She hoped that she would catch it, and she did! Everybody cheered. Sasha smiled.

"Hooray!" shouted the children.

Sasha passed the hat forward. She was happy to help. And one by one the students passed the hat to Ranger Bill in the front of the boat.

"Thank you very much," said Ranger Bill to Sasha. "Would you like to come up to the front of the boat for the rest of the ride?" asked Ranger Bill. "It must be very hard to hear back there."

"Yes, it is, thank you," said Sasha. She made her way carefully to the <u>bow</u> of the boat. Maybe the pond wasn't so bad after all.

1 What is this story mostly about?

○ The front of the boat

○ How Ranger Bill lost his hat in the river

○ How Sasha feels about seeing the turtle

○ What happens when Sasha goes on a boat trip

2 How did Ranger Bill feel when he discovered his hat had fallen in the river?

○ Excited

○ Confused

○ Worried

○ Happy

3 In this story, the word <u>bow</u> means —

○ branch

○ motor

○ front

○ hat

4 Why was Sasha upset when she got off the bus?

○ She didn't want to go on the boat ride.

○ She ate too many hot dogs.

○ The bus ride was too long and she felt a little sick.

○ She didn't want to go to school.

5 How did Sasha feel after she passed the hat?

○ Pleased

○ Unhappy

○ Disappointed

○ Afraid

6 When did Ranger Bill lose his hat?

○ When a branch hit it

○ When the wind blew it off

○ During a rain storm

○ While he was eating lunch

Directions: Read the story. Then read each question about the story. Choose the best answer to the question. Mark the space for the answer you have chosen.

Who was Helen Keller?

Helen Keller was a person who faced major challenges in her life. Helen became deaf and blind when she was two years old. Although she was deaf and blind, she still learned to talk. Helen learned "sign language," which is a way of speaking with your hands. Later, Helen learned how to write. She also learned to speak with her voice. As an adult, she helped many other deaf and blind people learn to do the same things.

Helen Keller was born in Alabama in 1880. Her family was very caring. Her parents did everything that they could to help her. Helen's sister was her close companion.

Anne Sullivan was Helen's teacher. Anne came to live with Helen when Helen was seven years old. It was Anne who showed Helen how to make letters by making shapes with Helen's fingers. Anne made a different shape with Helen's fingers for each letter of the alphabet. Anne also used Helen's sense of touch to help her learn new words. Anne did this by putting Helen's hand in some water. Then she showed Helen how to spell w-a-t-e-r with her fingers. Anne did this

with as many things as possible. After many months, Helen understood how to use the finger movements to talk with other people. Because she knew sign language, Helen was pleased to be able to talk with many interesting people. When Helen was ten years old, she learned to speak with her voice, too. It took a lot of hard work because she could not hear her own voice. But she never gave up.

When Helen was older, she had a special typewriter. Instead of typing letters, it made bumps in patterns on paper. These patterns make the letters of an alphabet called Braille. Many blind people learn to read these patterns with their fingers. Today, thousands of books are printed in Braille.

Helen learned to read Braille. She also learned to write with her typewriter. It provided her with another way of communicating.

Helen went to college when she was twenty years old. She worked very hard at her schoolwork. She finished college in 1904. For the rest of her life, Helen Keller used what she had learned to help other blind and deaf people.

1 The word <u>provided</u> in this story means —

   ○ asked

   ○ gave

   ○ took

   ○ kept

2 How did Anne Sullivan probably feel about Helen Keller?

   ○ Unhappy

   ○ Angry

   ○ Jealous

   ○ Proud

3 What is the main idea of this story?

   ○ Helen Keller became deaf when she was two years old.

   ○ Helen Keller went to live with Anne Sullivan.

   ○ Helen Keller worked hard to learn to read and to write.

   ○ Helen Keller traveled to many different countries.

4 Where was Helen Keller born?

   ○ Mississippi

   ○ Alabama

   ○ Alaska

   ○ Florida

5 How did Helen Keller probably feel when she learned how to use sign language to talk with other people?

   ○ She did not like it.

   ○ She was happy.

   ○ She was angry.

   ○ She did not know she understood.

6 Which is a FACT in this story?

   ○ Helen Keller went to a famous school.

   ○ Helen Keller was forced to move.

   ○ Helen Keller never learned to read.

   ○ Helen Keller went to college.

Introduction

Welcome to *5 Days to the TAAS Reading Test!*

This part of the workbook is designed to help you and your teacher get ready for the TAAS reading test. All year you have been building your reading skills. Soon you will have a chance to put your skills to work.

During the week before the test, we will help you do two different things.

- First, we will teach you about the TAAS. You will take a practice reading test so you can learn about the test. We will show you the kinds of stories and questions that are on the real test. We will also give you some helpful hints about how to do your best on the test.

- Second, we will help you review some of the reading skills that you have already learned. You will learn how to use these skills to help you on the TAAS, and what you can do to perform your best on the test.

Once you have taken a practice test, learned about the TAAS, and reviewed your reading skills, you will be all set for the real test. As your teacher works with you on these assignments, be sure to ask your teacher any questions that you have about the test.

The TAAS is an important test that is designed to show you and your teacher how much you have learned this year. If you work hard this week, you will be ready for success on the TAAS.

Remember, always do your best!

Directions: Read the story. Then read each question about the story. Choose the best answer to the question. Mark the space for the answer you have chosen.

SAMPLE

The Flower Shop

"Come on in," said Heather as she opened the door to the flower shop. "The <u>lilies</u> look beautiful today."

"We should be able to get some nice flowers for Mother," said Gina.

Tomorrow is Mother's birthday. Heather and Gina wanted to buy flowers to surprise her.

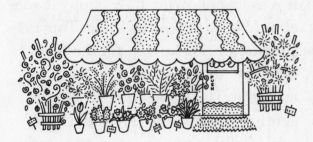

SD-1 The word <u>lilies</u> in this story means a kind of —

○ tree

○ party

○ flower

○ food

SD-2 Who were Heather and Gina buying flowers for?

○ Their sister

○ An uncle

○ Their mother

○ Their grandfather

STOP

Carlos Works on the Horse Farm

Carlos woke up as the sun rose. He looked out the window of the bedroom and saw the tall grass waving in the field next to the house. Carlos was excited about visiting his aunt and uncle for a week on their ranch in Wyoming. Carlos lived in a large city in New Jersey. He had never been on a farm. Aunt Maria and Uncle Tomas had a special kind of farm. They raised horses. Carlos slipped on his clothes and tennis shoes and went out to the kitchen. Aunt Maria was making pancakes for breakfast.

Uncle Tomas came in the kitchen. "Would you like to help me with the horses today?" he asked. "After you finish breakfast, take this bag of grain and fill the buckets that are hanging on the door of each horse stall."

"Sure," said Carlos. He sat down to eat. When he was done, he picked up the heavy bag and walked across the yard to the horse barn. Each horse had its own stall. The stalls were like large closets. The doors on the stalls only went halfway up. Some of the horses were looking out of the open part above the door. As Carlos stepped up to the first stall, the horse inside stamped its feet. It tossed its large head and snorted loudly. Carlos stepped back quickly. His hands started to shake.

"This is harder than I thought it would be," Carlos thought to himself. "How am I going to get close enough to fill the bucket?" Carlos stepped back up to the stall door. He looked closely at the horse in the stall. "Don't you want to eat?" he asked the horse.

"I'm sure that horse is hungry," said Uncle Tomas as he walked into the barn. He had been watching to make sure that Carlos was all right. "Let me show you."

"Thank you!" said Carlos.

Uncle Tomas showed Carlos how to speak softly to the horse as he filled the bucket. Carlos learned that the horse was not trying to scare him. It was just showing how happy it was about being fed. After Uncle Tomas showed Carlos how to fill the feed buckets, he let Carlos give the horse an apple. The horse took the apple gently with its large teeth. Carlos smiled and the horse seemed to smile back at him.

After they finished with the horses, Uncle Tomas and Carlos walked back to the house. "That wasn't so bad," said Carlos.

"You did a good job," said Uncle Tomas. "We'll make a horse farmer out of you in no time!"

Go on

1 Who asked Carlos to feed the horses?

○ Aunt Maria

○ Carlos's mother

○ Uncle Tomas

○ Carlos's father

2 Which of these happened last in this story?

○ Carlos woke up as the sun rose.

○ Carlos went to the horse barn.

○ Carlos and Uncle Tomas filled the feed buckets.

○ Carlos put on his tennis shoes.

3 Carlos's hands started to shake because —

○ Aunt Maria called him to breakfast

○ the horse scared him

○ the horse barn was very small

○ Uncle Tomas spoke to him

4 Tomorrow Carlos will probably —

○ go fishing

○ learn about cows

○ make pancakes for breakfast

○ feed the horses again

5 At the beginning of the story, how did Carlos feel about spending a week at his aunt and uncle's farm?

○ Tired

○ Happy

○ Confused

○ Proud

6 In this story, which of these is a FACT?

○ Uncle Tomas had more cows than horses.

○ Carlos is spending a week on the farm with his aunt and uncle.

○ The horses run very fast.

○ Carlos fed the horses in the evening.

Go on

July 8

Dear Diary,

Today was a crazy day! Mom and I went grocery shopping this morning. When we returned home, she gave me her keys to open the front door. We carried the groceries in and I helped Mom put them away. Then I went to my room to work on a puzzle.

Later this afternoon, Mom came into my room. "Would you like to go to the bookstore with me?" she asked. I said that it sounded like a great idea. Then she asked where her keys were.

I know I looked <u>stunned</u>. I could not remember where I had put the keys. Mom and I started to look for them.

Mom said that she would look in the kitchen. She told me to look in my bedroom.

"Make sure you look on the floor," said Mom. I looked on the floor, and under the bed. I even looked under the pillows on my bed. Mom checked all the kitchen counters. She did not find the keys. "I guess we can't go to the bookstore until Daddy gets home with the spare car keys," said Mom. I was concerned.

Since we were not going anywhere, I decided to get some milk and cookies. That is when it happened. I opened the refrigerator. You won't believe what I found next to the milk. That is right, I found the keys!

Caroline M.

Go on

7 The word <u>stunned</u> in this story means —

- ○ happy
- ○ angry
- ○ shocked
- ○ excited

8 This story is mostly about —

- ○ going to the bookstore
- ○ finding the keys
- ○ eating cookies
- ○ putting away groceries

9 Caroline first looked for the keys —

- ○ in her kitchen
- ○ in the refrigerator
- ○ in the car
- ○ on her bedroom floor

10 How did Caroline feel when she could not find the keys?

- ○ Angry
- ○ Pleased
- ○ Proud
- ○ Worried

Go on

Rugby

Rugby football is an exciting, fast-moving game that is played all over the world. It started in Great Britain and is like American football in many ways. Rugby is a tough sport. Its players are strong and fast. Men, women, older boys, and older girls in many countries play rugby. It is not usually played by young children since the playing can be rough.

Rugby is played with two teams of 15 players each. A rugby field is 100 meters long. There are goalposts at each end of the field. Behind each of the goalposts is the "in-goal" area. The rugby ball is a leather ball that is filled with air. It is 28 to 29 centimeters long and looks a little like an American football.

In rugby, a team attempts to score by moving the ball into the other team's in-goal area. The other team tries to take the ball away and to move it to the opposite in-goal area. A team receives four points when they successfully move the ball into the appropriate in-goal area. After a team scores, it can get two more points by kicking the ball into the in-goal area. The team with the most points at the end of the game wins.

A rugby game is played in two halves. Each half is 40 minutes long. During the game, players can move the ball by running with it, kicking it, or throwing it. However, a player cannot throw the ball forward. Players can only throw the ball sideways or backwards to another player on their team. Members of the opposing team try to stop the person with the ball by knocking that player down. This is called a <u>tackle</u>. A tackled player must let the ball go so another player can pick it up.

Different team members have different jobs to do. Each team has <u>forwards</u> and backs. The forwards try to get the ball from the other team by tackling. When the forwards get the ball, they throw it to the backs. The backs move the ball toward the goal. Referees stay on the field and watch the game to make sure that all players follow the rules.

When a rugby team does not follow the rules of the game, the other team gets to take a penalty kick. If the game is stopped for some reason, it is usually started again with a scrum. In a scrum, players from each team link arms and form a close circle. A referee throws the ball into the middle of the circle and the players try to kick it out to their side of the field.

Although rugby players do not wear helmets or pads for protection, they do wear special shoes. Their shoes have

Go on

metal spikes on the bottom. Rugby players usually play in shorts, a long-sleeved shirt, and knee-length socks.

Rugby is a tough and difficult sport. But once you learn the rules, it is fun to play and to watch. If you want an exciting time, find a rugby game.

11 In this story, the <u>forwards</u> are —
○ the areas behind the goalposts
○ a way to knock a player down
○ special long-sleeved shirts
○ players who get the ball from the other team

12 The word <u>tackle</u> in this story means —
○ knock down the player who has the ball
○ throw the ball to another player
○ run down the field with the ball
○ start the game with a scrum

13 Rugby can be played by —
○ only people in Great Britain
○ women only
○ boys only
○ older children and adults

14 The only special equipment rugby players wear is —
○ helmets
○ pads
○ shin guards
○ spiked shoes

15 This story is mostly about —
○ how rugby is played
○ what rugby players wear
○ the number of players on a rugby team
○ the size of a rugby field

Go on

Always Find the Best

Many years ago, there was a young girl named Eleanor. Eleanor's parents had died when she was very young and she had lived with her great-grandfather ever since. Eleanor was a happy child because her great-grandfather taught her that no matter how bad things might seem, there is always a good reason to be happy. Eleanor practiced this game and could always find some reason to be glad.

One day, Eleanor's great-grandfather died. She moved far away to live with her mother's cousin Francie. Francie was a <u>grim</u> woman. She was sad and serious and did not have many friends. When she was younger, she had been happily in love with the town's dogcatcher. Unfortunately, they had a terrible fight and Francie said that she would never speak to him again. She had been unhappy ever since.

Eleanor's new room was small and dark. There was a very tall tree outside her window. It blocked all of the sunlight from coming into the room. Eleanor missed her warm, old room at her great-grandfather's house. She sat down on her hard bed and felt lonely and sad. As she thought of her great-grandfather, she knew that he would be disappointed if she forgot how to find the best thing about this situation. She thought of some reason to be happy about the ugly room. She said to Francie, "Thank you for a room with bare walls. It means that I will have to look out my window to see all of the birds that live in the big tree. I'd rather look at the birds than at pictures on my wall."

Francie was surprised by Eleanor. She had not thought that such a young child could have such a pleasant way of looking at things. "What a wonderful child," she said to herself.

As Eleanor met new people in town, she began to make many friends. She taught them her game. Soon, the whole town knew about the special gift that Eleanor had brought.

One day, Eleanor's neighbors came over to ask for her help. Their dog, Kilo, had gotten loose and could not be found. Eleanor adored Kilo and was very worried that he might be hurt if he wasn't found soon. She and Francie headed out to check the road to town. After a little while, Eleanor and Francie found Kilo.

Just as Eleanor and Francie were taking Kilo back home, the dogcatcher drove up in his buggy. He hopped out and offered to give the ladies a ride home. Francie did not look happy to see the dogcatcher. She looked down and refused to answer him.

"You know, Francie," the dogcatcher said slowly. "I'm sorry that we had that awful argument all of those years ago. Will you accept my apology?" The dogcatcher looked truly sad. He walked over to a wild rose bush and picked off a flower. When he handed it to Francie, she looked up at him.

"Oh, Samuel," she said. "You're right. I've wasted far too much time being angry at you. I accept your apology."

Eleanor, Francie, Kilo, and the dogcatcher climbed into the buggy. Eleanor could not believe what a difference she saw in Francie. Everyone smiled all of the way home.

Go on

© McGraw-Hill School Division

16 In this story, the word <u>grim</u> means —

   ○ unhappy

   ○ wise

   ○ lazy

   ○ delighted

17 What is this story mostly about?

   ○ Kilo getting lost

   ○ Eleanor's new life with Francie

   ○ A ride in the dogcatcher's buggy

   ○ The big tree outside of Eleanor's room

18 How does Eleanor feel when she first sees her room at Francie's house?

   ○ Amazed

   ○ Angry

   ○ Sad

   ○ Curious

19 Which of these is a FACT in this story?

   ○ Kilo gets loose.

   ○ Eleanor and Francie rode their bikes.

   ○ The dogcatcher was unhelpful.

   ○ Eleanor's room was painted blue.

20 What is the main idea of this story?

   ○ Eleanor was sad because her room was small and dark.

   ○ Francie was an unhappy woman who needed company.

   ○ Finding something good in every situation can make people happy.

   ○ The dogcatcher always drove his buggy.

21 The dogcatcher says that he is —

   ○ going to have to take Kilo to the pound

   ○ very good at his job

   ○ afraid that it will rain

   ○ sorry about the argument

22 Which of these is a FACT in this story?

   ○ Eleanor's great-grandfather died.

   ○ Francie loved the town sheriff.

   ○ Eleanor lived in a very large city.

   ○ The dogcatcher picked a daisy.

23 How does Samuel make Francie feel when he gives her a flower?

   ○ Lonely

   ○ Unsure

   ○ Tired

   ○ Happy

Go on

The Olympic Games

Every four years, athletes from all over the world come together for the Olympic games. The Olympics are a time for people from many countries to compete for prizes and get to know each other.

Pierre de Coubertin started the first Olympic games in 1896 in Athens, Greece. Mr. Coubertin was a teacher in France. He had learned about a contest that had often taken place over two thousand years before in Greece. Men would come from all over to run races in a city called Olympia. Mr. Coubertin believed that countries would not start wars if the people from those countries became friends. He thought that starting the Olympic games would be a good way to encourage those kinds of friendships.

Now each time that the Olympics take place, they are held in a different country. Only two hundred and eighty-five men from sixteen countries competed in the sports in the first Olympics. Today more than ten thousand men and women from over one hundred and sixty countries participate in the Olympic games.

The Olympic games are divided into Winter Olympics and Summer Olympics. The Summer Olympic games have sports such as running, basketball, ping-pong, horseback riding, and soccer. Water sports such as swimming and diving are also a big part of the Summer games.

The Winter games are held in a country with lots of snow. Winter sports such as skiing, snowboarding, ice hockey, and ice-skating <u>require</u> very cold weather. Because the Winter games need ice and snow, they are held in a cold month such as January or February.

The Olympic games always begin with a special parade. All of the athletes who will be competing in the games march in the parade and represent their country. Several athletes from each country carry their country's flag. Bands play music that comes from many different places around the world. Children dance and sometimes doves are set free into the air as a sign of peace. At the end of the parade, a runner brings in a torch of fire. The runner uses the torch to light a fire in a large bowl. This fire is kept burning until the end of the games.

Athletes work very hard to get ready for the games. They practice every day for many years. It is a great honor to be part of the athletic teams that compete at the Olympics. At the end of each <u>competition</u>, the top three winners get special medals. The medals are gold, silver, and bronze. The winners stand on a platform while music plays and flags are waved. These winners are very happy that they won for their countries.

Go on

24 In this story, the word <u>require</u> means —

   ○ play

   ○ work

   ○ need

   ○ swim

25 In this story, the word <u>competition</u> means —

   ○ a place to run

   ○ a game for prizes

   ○ a person who loses

   ○ a country at war

26 About how many athletes take part in the Olympic games each year?

   ○ Ten thousand

   ○ Five hundred

   ○ Twenty

   ○ Five

27 Ice hockey is a —

   ○ very cold country

   ○ summer sport

   ○ kind of parade

   ○ winter sport

28 What is the main idea of this story?

   ○ Snow usually falls in January and February.

   ○ The Olympic games bring people from many countries together.

   ○ Athens is a city in Greece.

   ○ Swimming is part of the Summer Olympics.

29 Mr. Coubertin started the Olympic games because —

   ○ he wanted to know how to ski

   ○ he wanted people all over the world to be friends

   ○ he found a gold medal

   ○ he liked parades

30 How do winners in the Olympic games probably feel?

   ○ Unhappy

   ○ Careful

   ○ Proud

   ○ Confused

Go on

Where did Miguel and Matt go for spring vacation?

When the car finally stopped, Miguel and Matt jumped out before Miguel's parents could even get their doors opened. The boys stood looking at the waves that were crashing on the beach. Matt had come with Miguel's family for a vacation at the coast. "The water is beautiful," said Matt. "I'm glad I'm here."

"I knew you'd like it," said Miguel. "Let's go for a swim."

Miguel's mother showed the boys the changing rooms where they could put on their swimsuits. After they had their suits on, they started down to the water's edge. They walked <u>cautiously</u> to avoid the sharp shells that covered the beach. Miguel's father was right behind them.

Miguel waded into the water right away. "How deep is it out there?" asked Matt.

"It does not get deep until you get far away from the beach," said Miguel. "Come on in."

"Isn't it cold?" asked Matt. "I'm not sure I want to get in."

"You can do it," replied Miguel. "You just have to run and get in fast before you change your mind. The water isn't too cold."

Matt made his decision. He took a deep breath and then ran as fast as he could into the clear, turquoise water. He did not stop until the water was up to his knees. He splashed the cool water up onto his face. "The water feels great," said Matt. "I love the ocean! Can we go in deeper?"

"Sure," said Miguel. "Dad said that we could go out until the water is up to our waists. He's right over there watching to make sure that we are all right. This is going to be a really fun day!"

Go on

31 When the story says the boys walked <u>cautiously</u>, it means that they walked —

- ○ angrily
- ○ quickly
- ○ sadly
- ○ carefully

32 What happened first?

- ○ The boys changed into their swimsuits.
- ○ Matt got into the water.
- ○ Matt and Miguel got out of the car.
- ○ The boys walked down to the water.

33 What will Matt and Miguel probably do next?

- ○ Keep playing in the ocean
- ○ Ride their bikes
- ○ Eat lunch
- ○ Play cards

34 How did Matt feel before he got into the water?

- ○ Excited
- ○ Concerned
- ○ Careful
- ○ Tired

35 Which sentence tells something make-believe?

- ○ Matt and Miguel tried not to step on sharp shells.
- ○ Matt rode on a mermaid.
- ○ Miguel's parents watched the boys swim.
- ○ Matt went with Miguel to swim in the ocean.

36 This story is mostly about —

- ○ Matt and Miguel's day at the beach
- ○ putting on swimsuits
- ○ walking carefully through the sand
- ○ a long car trip

END OF PRACTICE TEST

What do I need to know about the TAAS reading test?

The TAAS reading test is untimed.

- You have as much time as you need, so you should always answer every question. If you get frustrated, bored, or lose your focus, just take a deep breath. Then relax and continue working.

- You will read approximately six stories. Then you will answer between four and eight questions after each story. You will have 36 questions total that you will have to answer. Work carefully and take your time.

- If you come to a question that seems really hard, just do your best to answer it. Then go on to the next question. Don't let yourself get stuck for too long. We will go over some ways that can help you answer a question when you're not sure how to answer it.

There is no penalty for guessing on the TAAS reading test.

- You should always do your best to answer a question. Start by putting an X at the end of as many wrong answers as you can. If you are not able to narrow the choices to just one answer, you should take your best guess. You can only gain points!

Ruling Out Wrong Answers

On a test like the TAAS, your job is to find the *best* answer to each question. The best answer might not always be the answer that you think is right. But, it will always be the best answer from what the story tells you. After you read the questions, read the story again. Look for the part of the story that will help you answer the questions. When you find information that you think answers a question, read the question again. Try to answer the question in your own words before you look at the answer choices. Then read the choices and find the best one given what you have read in the story.

If you have trouble finding the answer, or if you aren't sure which answer is the *best*, ruling out bad answer choices can help you find the best answer. Read each answer choice carefully to see if it is a good answer choice to the question. If it is not, then get rid of that answer choice by putting an X after it.

The X will remind you that you **do not** think that the answer choice is a good one. Answering the questions this way will help you find all of the answer choices you know are **wrong**. What will be left will be the choice or choices that you think best answer the question. Then you can choose the best one of the choices that you haven't X-ed out. **Remember, the best answer is always based on the information in the story.**

Try this:

> "You're finished already?" Millie's mother asked the plumber. "That didn't take long at all. I'm amazed."

How did Millie's mother feel when she discovered the plumber was finished?

- O Lonely
- O Worried
- O Surprised
- O Afraid

Looking at this question, you might not know right away what the *best* answer is. However, when you look at the answer choices, you might know which answers are wrong. Place an X after the answer choices that you know are wrong.

When Millie's mother said, "You're finished already?" in the story, do you think she was—

Lonely?	No.	Eliminate it by putting an X after the word.
Worried?	No.	Eliminate it by putting an X after the word.
Surprised?	Yes.	Leave it.
Afraid?	No.	Eliminate it by putting an X after the word.

Remember, sometimes ruling out wrong answers will help you get rid of all but one answer choice. Other times, it will help to get rid of two or three answers. In those cases, after you have placed an X after the wrong answers, you can make a good guess from the choices that are left.

Reading the Passage Actively

Imagine that your grandparents are coming to visit, and they are going to stay in your bedroom. Your parents tell you that you'll have to clean your room and get all of your stuff off the floor. Your father says he will help you. He gets some boxes, and he puts your things into the boxes.

Then your father starts to put the boxes into your closet. "Wait," you say. "How will I know where everything is?" He tells you that you can label the boxes by writing on the outside of each one. You look inside each box and decide how to label it. Before you write on the box, you want to make sure that your label will tell you what is in it.

In this box, you see your in-line skates, ballet slippers, dress shoes, and ice-skates.

What will you write on this box so you will know what's in it?

shoes
_____

In this box, you see all your notes, letters, cards, and old schoolwork.

What will you write on this box?
_____

In this box, you see all your video games and board games.

What will you write on this box?
_____

In the same way, you can label each paragraph in the stories you read on the TAAS. You want to be able to go back to the story and find the answer to a question quickly. You don't want to have to search through every paragraph — just like you don't want to search through every box. The words you write next to each paragraph must tell you about what is in the paragraph.

As you're reading each paragraph, come up with one or two words that remind you of what you read in the paragraph. This is called labeling. After you read each paragraph, ask yourself, "What did I just read about?" Just like when you labeled what was in the boxes, you're going to label the side of the paragraph. Write the words that remind you of what the paragraph said.

Let's practice labeling paragraphs.

Annie's mother brought home a little puppy for Annie's birthday. Annie was very excited to become friends with the little dog. He was so cute! He had fluffy brown fur and big, shiny eyes. His tail wagged back and forth.

What words will you write next to this paragraph so that you will remember what is in it?

_____

Annie named her new puppy Scout. But, when she went over to pet Scout, the little puppy hid under the table. Annie was sad.

What will you write next to this paragraph?

_____

"You need to be patient, Annie," said her mother. "Scout is new here. He will need some time to get used to us. He's just a little dog. Everyone must seem so big to him!"

What will you write next to this paragraph?

_____

Now when you answer the questions, the labels will help you find the answers to the questions more quickly.

Which of these happened first?

- ○ Annie named her puppy Scout.

- ○ Annie's mother told her to be patient.

- ○ Annie got a puppy for her birthday.

- ○ Scout hid under the table.

Practice: Reading the Passage Actively

Read the story. Label each paragraph with one or two words about the paragraph.

Archery

Archery is the sport of shooting arrows from a bow. It is a sport that has been around for a long time. The first archery contest was in England in 1673. However, bows and arrows were used for hunting for many years before that. Many people think that the ancient Egyptians were the first people to use a bow and arrow.

The bow is usually made out of wood or some other strong substance. It is bent into a curved shape. A strong string is then tied from one end of the bow to the other. The string is pulled very tight before it is tied. The bow looks like the letter "D" after the string is attached.

The arrow is made from a straight piece of wood. It has a metal-covered point on one end. Cut feathers are attached to the arrow at the other end. These feathers help the arrow fly through the air. At the very end of the arrow near the feathers, there is a notch cut into the arrow. This is where the string of the bow fits into the arrow.

An archer is a person who shoots the arrows. The archer puts the string of the bow into the notch in the arrow. Then the archer pulls the arrow back. The arrow flies through the air when the archer lets go of the string.

There are different kinds of archery contests. The most common contest is to shoot arrows at a target. The target is usually made up of a large circle. There are four smaller circles inside of it. The circles are placed one on top of the other like rings. Each one is a different size. The smallest circle is in the center of all of them and is called the "bull's-eye."

The colors of the rings are always the same. The bull's-eye is yellow, and the other rings from the center outward are red, blue, black, and white. Each ring is worth a set number of points. Since the bull's-eye is the smallest, it is the hardest to hit.

An archer wears a leather glove on the fingers that pull the string. This protects the fingers from being hurt by the string. An archer also wears a leather pad on the arm that holds the bow. This pad protects the archer's arm from the string of the bow. When the arrow is released, the string snaps back into place. Without the arm pad on, the string might hurt the archer.

Archery takes a lot of skill. It takes practice to shoot an arrow so that it hits the bull's-eye. Because arrows have sharp points, only people who are closely watched by an adult or who know how to shoot an arrow safely should try this sport. This means that archers must train with a teacher for many years before they can practice on their own.

Practice: Reading the Passage Actively

Read the story. Label each paragraph with one or two words about the paragraph.

Alexander Graham Bell

People have been using one of Alexander Graham Bell's inventions, the telephone, for more than 150 years. But, Alexander Graham Bell is famous for more than just the telephone. Many people know him because of his work with deaf people. During his life, Bell taught many deaf people how to speak.

Alexander Graham Bell was born in Scotland in 1847. He moved to the United States in 1871. His father had worked with deaf people for many years. Bell decided that he would do the same thing. He began to teach deaf people how to talk. He used his father's ideas to show deaf students how to make sound. It was a new way for deaf people to learn how to talk.

Alexander Graham Bell's goal was to help deaf people. In 1872, he started a school for deaf people. He continued to use his father's ideas at his school. With them, he was able to teach people how to talk even though they could not hear him. His most famous student was Helen Keller.

People liked Alexander Graham Bell because he was a caring person. He tried to learn more about deafness. He also tried to find out why some people are born deaf. He even invented a machine that measured how much a person could hear.

Although he is most famous for his invention of the telephone, Alexander Graham Bell invented many other things, too. He invented a kite that was large enough to carry a person. He even designed a boat that traveled above the water. It moved at 70 miles per hour and was the fastest boat at that time.

Vocabulary In Context Questions

Some of the questions on the TAAS reading test will ask you about a word that is underlined in the story. Sometimes you will know what the underlined word means. Other times you will have to look for a clue to figure out what the word means. The clue words are usually *near* the underlined word.

> Mrs. Murphy asked me to help with the <u>decorations</u>. She said I could decide where the balloons and ribbons should go.

While you might not know what the word <u>decorations</u> means, the sentence that comes after it talks about balloons and ribbons. This is a clue. Balloons and ribbons are kinds of decorations.

Sometimes you will not find the clue right away. Just remember — there is **always** a clue. When you have difficulty finding the clues, you will have to look more closely at the sentences or words around the underlined word. Sometimes the clue is *before* the underlined word. Sometimes it is *after* the underlined word.

Now try this example.

> Karen held the garden hose. She let the water run into the dirt around the tree she had just planted. The dirt was <u>soaked</u>.

In this story, <u>soaked</u> means —

- ○ wet
- ○ dirty
- ○ shady
- ○ busy

Don't forget to rule out wrong answers!

Here's another example.

> The Native Americans who lived on Cape Cod used a special trap to catch fish. It was called a <u>weir</u>. A weir is a stone wall built out into the water. At the end of the wall is a net. As the fish try to pass by the wall, they get caught in the net.

In this story, a weir is —

- ○ a fishing pole
- ○ a house
- ○ a Native American
- ○ a trap

Most people don't know what the word <u>weir</u> means. But, if you read carefully, you will notice some clues that tell you what a <u>weir</u> is.

When you look at the answer choices, place an X after each answer choice that you know is wrong.

Could a <u>weir</u> be —

a fishing pole?	No.	Why? Even though a <u>weir</u> is used to catch fish, the story never talked about a fishing pole. Put an X after the word.
a house?	No.	Why? The story never talked about a house. Put an X after the word.
a Native American?	No.	Why? Even though the story talked about a Native American, the <u>weir</u> is not a Native American. Go back to the story and double check this. Put an X after the word.
a trap?	Yes!	Why? The story says that a <u>weir</u> is "a special trap." Fill in the answer bubble.

Name: _____ **Date:** _____

Find the clue words in the story below.

> Ambulance workers have a very exciting job. Some ambulance workers are <u>volunteers.</u> Volunteers are not paid for their work in the ambulance. They usually give their time and work for free.

Write down the clue words from the story on the lines below.

_____

_____

_____

Use the clue words that you found to help you understand the meaning of the underlined word.

In this story, a <u>volunteer</u> is someone who —

- ○ enjoys puzzles
- ○ studies ambulances
- ○ likes good food
- ○ works without pay

The underlined word will sometimes seem very hard. Remember to look for the clues and to rule out answer choices that you know are wrong.

Try another example.

> Karl and Anne went into the kitchen. All of the <u>ingredients</u> were on the counter. They had everything they needed to make a cake. They had butter, milk, sugar, flour, and eggs.

In this story, <u>ingredients</u> are —

- ○ things you use to make a cake
- ○ different kinds of butter
- ○ things that are in the kitchen sink
- ○ forks and spoons

© McGraw-Hill School Division

Practice: Vocabulary In Context Questions

Read each story selection. Then read the question. Choose the best answer to the question. Mark the space for the answer you have chosen.

> "Do you still sell the meatball sandwich?" Daniel asked. "I had it last week and it was <u>delicious</u>. It was the best sandwich I've ever had."

The word <u>delicious</u> in this story means —

- ○ tasty
- ○ hot
- ○ terrible
- ○ dangerous

> Pulling weeds wasn't as easy as Mara had expected it to be. Sometimes the leaves broke off, and the roots stayed in the ground. Mara's Aunt Clare gave her a <u>spade</u>. It was a special tool to help Mara dig the weeds out of the ground.

In this story, a <u>spade</u> is a —

- ○ root of a weed
- ○ tool for digging
- ○ special leaf on a weed
- ○ difficult job

> Mr. Gray noticed that the light bulb had burned out. He <u>replaced</u> it with a new one.

The word <u>replaced</u> in the story means —

- ○ showed
- ○ tried to hide
- ○ changed
- ○ did not try

Practice: Vocabulary In Context Questions

Read each story selection. Then read the question. Choose the best answer to the question. Mark the space for the answer you have chosen.

> A newspaper office has many different kinds of people working for it. Editors, reporters, proofreaders, printers, and delivery teams all work for the newspaper. Together they <u>guarantee</u> that the newspaper lands on your front porch every morning.

The word <u>guarantee</u> in this story means —

- O say out loud
- O deliver
- O make sure
- O make it impossible

> Lisa was going to be in her first piano <u>recital</u>. She would be playing the piano on Sunday afternoon for many people. She was very nervous. Lisa had only played the piano for her parents and her teacher. This time, all of Mrs. Livingstone's students and their families would be there.

In this story, a <u>recital</u> is a—

- O drama
- O walk
- O bench
- O concert

> Rain can sometimes change the speed of the river water. When it rains there is more water in the river than usual. This causes the river water to move <u>swiftly</u>. After the storm, the river water will slow down to its normal speed.

In this story, the word <u>swiftly</u> means—

- O heavily
- O quickly
- O slowly
- O widely

MORE Practice: Vocabulary In Context Questions

> Cocoa seeds have to be <u>processed</u> before they are good to eat. The seeds must be dried and cooked. Then they are mixed with sugar and oil and milk to make them taste better.

The word <u>processed</u> in this story means —

○ changed

○ eaten

○ salted

○ tasted

> Firefighters are <u>trained</u> to be calm even when the situation is dangerous. Being calm lets them help people and save lives.

In this story, <u>trained</u> means—

○ surprised

○ watched

○ taught

○ left

> Herbert watched the planes taking off from the airport. He saw one plane drive slowly across the <u>runway</u> and he pointed to it. "Is that the plane that we'll fly on?" he asked his brother.

The word <u>runway</u> in this story means the —

○ road that airplanes drive on

○ wings on the airplane

○ person who flies the airplane

○ windows in the airport

© McGraw-Hill School Division

Supporting Ideas Questions

For every question on the TAAS reading test, it is very important that you look back to the story to find the *best* answer. Even when you *think* you know the answer, it is **always** a good idea to look back at the story. Since the TAAS reading test is **not** timed, you have all the time you need. Read the story, read the question, and then go back to the story to find the information that you need.

Detail Questions

One way to keep track of important details in the story is to label the paragraphs. This will help you to find answers quickly. Once you find the part of the story that you need, underline the information you find. This will help you focus on that information. It will also make it easy to find it again if you need to.

Let's practice finding details in a story. Label each of the steps in the story.

BUILD A WOODLAND TERRARIUM

1. In a clear glass or plastic tank put in these layers in this order: charcoal, gravel, sand, and soil.   _____

2. Collect plant samples. Add rocks, sticks, and pinecones.   _____

3. Add any small animals you can collect (especially worms, salamanders, crickets, and spiders).   _____

4. Cover the tank.   _____

5. Make a record of what you have done by drawing a picture of the layers. Label each layer.   _____

Now answer this question by finding the part of the story that tells you the answer, and underlining the information in the story when you find it.

You can make a record of what you have done by —

    ○ collecting worms

    ○ drawing a picture

    ○ adding pinecones

    ○ covering the tank

Setting Questions

Some stories ask you to look for clues that tell you **where** or **when** the story takes place. Sometimes this information is easy to find. Other times, you will need to use clues to figure it out.

The Third Grade of Thomas Jefferson Elementary School proudly presents:

THE THREE THIEVES
Friday, May 13, at 7:00 p.m. in the auditorium
Snacks will be served in the cafeteria after the play.

CAST

Roxy Raccoon. . . . . .Jennifer Corrigan

Bobby Bear . . . . Michael Alonzo

Sandy Squirrel. . . . . Gina Huffington

Eric Elk. . . . . .Sidney Sanchez

Mr. Deerhide. . . . . .Andrew DiMarco

Mrs. Deerhide. . . . . .Abigail Krantz

Darren Deerhide. . . . . .Thomas Kean

Chorus members: Adam True, Betsy Grimble, and Lori Kiln.

In this play program, you can find many different pieces of information. It is hard to tell what is important, at first! When you go back to find the answers to these questions, underline the information you find.

1 The play takes place in the —

- O classroom
- O gym
- O cafeteria
- O auditorium

2 Lori Kiln helped with the play by —

- O making the costumes
- O playing the trombone
- O being Roxy Racoon
- O singing in the chorus

3 What will happen just after the play ends?

- O The actors will put on their costumes.
- O The chorus will practice.
- O Snacks will be served.
- O The stage will be decorated.

Following Directions Questions

Some of the questions on the TAAS will require you to follow directions that are found in the story. These stories sometimes look different from the story below, but they all ask you to **pay attention to the directions**.

Luka was very proud. His neighbor, Dr. Ward, chose him to look after Rudy, Dr. Ward's pet turtle. Dr. Ward left Luka a schedule to follow for the three weeks.

RUDY'S SCHEDULE, MAY 4 - 22:

ALWAYS REMEMBER:
- Turtles don't like to be too hot or too cold. Make sure the temperature in the room stays between 60 and 70 degrees.
- Please make sure Rudy always has lots of water.
- Rudy can eat only raw, clean vegetables or turtle food.

SCHEDULE:

MAY 4:   Rudy arrives. Keep his cage in a warm place.

MAY 5:   Feed Rudy and check his water.

MAY 8:   Change Rudy's water.

MAY 13:   Feed Rudy.

MAY 16:   Change Rudy's water and put in some new grass.

MAY 20:   Feed Rudy.

MAY 22:   Rudy returns to Dr. Ward.

---

1 Where should Luka keep Rudy?
   - ○ In the hot sun
   - ○ Outside in the cold
   - ○ In the refrigerator
   - ○ In a warm place

   Go back to the story and underline the part that tells you where Rudy should be kept.

2 According to the schedule, on what day should Luka put new grass in Rudy's cage?
   - ○ MAY 5
   - ○ MAY 13
   - ○ MAY 16
   - ○ MAY 20

   Find where the story talks about new grass. Underline what it says.

Sequence Questions

Sometimes questions on the TAAS ask you about **the order in which events occur**. Some will ask you which event happened *first*. Others will ask you which event happened *last*.

Travis went for a cross-country drive with his father. They drove through a place called the Painted Desert in the western part of the United States. Here are some things that Travis wrote in his diary about the trip:

June 15th

We are on our way to the Painted Desert. Dad said that the colors in the hills come from minerals that settled in the rocks millions of years ago. Dad also said that the desert is home to many interesting creatures. We saw a lizard and some birds. How do the animals live in this heat?

June 16th

Today we stopped in a little town called Winslow. The people were very friendly. There were only a few buildings in the whole town! We stopped in one building that was both a gas station and a grocery store. It sold all sorts of things, like bread and car tires!

June 17th

Today the hills and sand have turned into big, colored rocks! It's like someone took up a big paintbrush and brushed many colors of paint onto the rocks. The rocks are red and purple, light blue and yellow. I guess that's why they call it the Painted Desert! It's the most beautiful thing I've ever seen.

---

1 Which of these happened on June 15th?

   ○ Seeing the colored rocks

   ○ Visiting Winslow

   ○ Stopping in the grocery store

   ○ Seeing some animals

As you look at each answer choice, go back to the story and mark the information that you find. Then choose the only one that happened on the 15th.

2 Which of these happened last?

   ○ Seeing the colored rocks

   ○ Visiting Winslow

   ○ Stopping in the grocery store

   ○ Seeing some animals

As you look at each answer choice, go back to the story and mark the information that you find. Then choose the one that happened last.

Practice: Supporting Ideas Questions

Use all of the things that you have learned so far. Label the paragraphs, look for clues, and underline the details you find.

A Trip to the Bahamas

Joan and her Aunt Nancy usually spend time in the summer together. This year they decided to take a trip to the Bahamas. Joan kept a diary of their trip.

June 1st

I am so glad I am able to go on this trip with Aunt Nancy. Late this morning we got on the ship and found our room. It has a small bathroom and two beds. It is very nice. Our room is on the main deck, the floor that is above the water. There are four other decks below the water that have rooms just like ours. There is a dining room on the main deck. This is where we eat all of our meals. On the top floor there is a game room and lots of chairs for sitting in the sun. The bridge is also there. That is the room where the captain commands the ship. The name of our ship is the *Island Hopper*.

This afternoon we had a lifeboat drill. The people who work on the ship told us what to do. They said if the alarm sounds, everyone should follow these directions:

1.	Everyone must put on a life jacket. The life jackets are stored under your bed.
2.	Everyone must go to the main deck.
3.	From the main deck, everyone will go to the lifeboats with one of the crew.

June 2nd

We landed at Grand Bahama Island. Aunt Nancy says there are over 700 islands in the Bahamas. Only about 40 islands have people who live on them. It is a beautiful place. The beaches are covered with white sand. The ocean is different shades of blue and green. Aunt Nancy says the different colors show how deep the water is. Aunt Nancy and I walked along the beach and collected seashells. Then we rode a bus to Freeport. Freeport is the largest city on the island. There are so many stores! I bought a shirt for my brother.

June 3rd

Today we are going home. Being on a ship is so much fun. Aunt Nancy and I have already decided to take another cruise next summer!

© McGraw-Hill School Division

1 The word <u>deck</u> in this diary means —

- ○ island
- ○ floor
- ○ thoughts
- ○ meals

2 The word <u>bridge</u> in this diary means —

- ○ the ocean
- ○ where the captain works
- ○ the back of the ship
- ○ the dining room

3 Where is this diary being written?

- ○ On the beach
- ○ In Freeport
- ○ In Florida
- ○ On the ship

4 Which of these happened on June 2nd?

- ○ Walking on the beach
- ○ Having a lifeboat drill
- ○ Leaving Florida
- ○ Going scuba diving

5 If the ship's alarm sounds, you should —

- ○ go to the dining room
- ○ leave your life jacket under the bed
- ○ put your life jacket on
- ○ try to guess how deep the ocean is

6 About how many islands in the Bahamas have people living on them?

- ○ 40
- ○ 65
- ○ 700
- ○ 2000

7 Freeport is a —

- ○ ship
- ○ beach
- ○ shirt
- ○ city

8 Joan and Aunt Nancy ate lunch —

- ○ on the bridge
- ○ in the ship dining room
- ○ in Freeport
- ○ in the game room

Practice: Supporting Ideas Questions

Use all of the things that you have learned so far. Label the paragraphs, look for clues, and underline the details you find.

Corina Makes a Choice

Corina sat at her kitchen table eating breakfast. Two of her cereal boxes had advertisements on the back for different games. She was trying to decide which game to buy with her allowance. One was a math game. Corina was good at math and liked to solve math problems. She was also a good speller. The other game was a word game. There were lots of different ways it could be played to learn new words.

Order **MATH GAMES** today! Every month you will receive a new game with lots of math problems to solve.

In addition to the game and its rules, each month you will receive a story about a <u>mathematician</u>. It might be a math expert from the past or someone who is currently a math expert.

Each game will also include:

- Ways to play the game in teams or by yourself
- Game pieces you can collect

To order, send in the order form and the box top. Mail it today!

The **SPELLING BEE GAME** Do you like to spell? Do you like to learn new words? Then this is the game for you!

To order:

1. Fill out the form that is inside this box.

2. Cut out the picture of the SPELLING BEE GAME on the back of the box.

3. Tape the form and the picture together.

4. Mail them in an envelope.

First, you will receive a game board. Each month after that, you will receive a new game to play on the board. Some games will test your spelling. Other games will challenge you with new words. Move across the board as you use the new words correctly in a sentence! Each new word comes with a <u>definition</u> so you will know what it means. Each month you will also receive word puzzles and spelling tips.

Order Today!

1 In the ***MATH GAMES*** ad, a <u>mathematician</u> is someone who —

   ○ likes contests

   ○ is good at spelling

   ○ writes books

   ○ is an expert in math

2 Why would Corina like ***MATH GAMES***?

   ○ She thinks math tests are fun.

   ○ She likes to solve math problems.

   ○ She enjoys word puzzles.

   ○ She likes to win contests.

3 Where did Corina eat breakfast?

   ○ At school

   ○ In her math classroom

   ○ At her kitchen table

   ○ In the dining room

4 If Corina orders ***The SPELLING BEE GAME***, what will she get?

   ○ Stories about mathematicians

   ○ Math games

   ○ A game board

   ○ A math expert pen pal

5 If Corina wants to order ***MATH GAMES*** she should —

   ○ learn new spelling words

   ○ take another math class

   ○ send in the form and the box top

   ○ get a math book from the library

6 The word <u>definition</u> in this story means —

   ○ the meaning of a word

   ○ the name of the author

   ○ the winner of the contest

   ○ a list of spelling tips

7 Why would Corina like ***The SPELLING BEE GAME***?

   ○ She thinks spelling bees are fun.

   ○ She is a good speller.

   ○ She likes math contests.

   ○ She enjoys ordering games.

8 Where does this story mostly take place?

   ○ at school

   ○ Corina's friend's house

   ○ Corina's house

   ○ the backyard

Inference and Generalization Questions

Sometimes the story will tell you exactly how a character feels. Other times you will have to look for clues about how the character feels.

> Tania could hardly wait to go to class. Today was the day the animals would arrive! Maybe Tania would get to feed the chicks.

How did Tania feel about going to class?

- ○ Lonely
- ○ Happy
- ○ Sorry
- ○ Clever

HINT: Put an X after answers you know are wrong. Then pick the best answer.

Sometimes a character's feelings will change during the story. Some questions on the TAAS will ask you how a character feels at the *beginning* of the story. Other questions will ask you how a character feels at the *end* of the story.

> The beach was far from where Derek lived with his family, and they didn't get to go very often. One day, Derek's parents told him they would go to the beach the next weekend. Derek was very happy.

> When the day came to go to the beach, Derek woke up early. He heard a pattering at his bedroom window. At first, he wondered what it was. It sounded almost like... rain. Derek's heart sank.

At the end of the story, Derek probably feels —

- ○ tired
- ○ excited
- ○ sad
- ○ amazed

© McGraw-Hill School Division

Some stories on the TAAS will not tell you how a character feels about something. Questions about these kinds of stories will ask you to predict how a character probably feels about something or someone. These questions might even ask you how a character makes someone else feel.

> After lunch, Zachary rushed to the closet to get his coat. It wasn't there! He couldn't believe his eyes. He blinked and rubbed his eyes with his hands. He looked again. His coat was still not there. Zachary's eyes filled with tears, and he felt a lump in his throat.

How did Zachary feel when his coat wasn't in the closet?
- O   Amused
- O   Calm
- O   Pleased
- O   Upset

> Lou and his father went to the music store and bought Lou a red plastic recorder. As soon as they got home, Lou took the recorder out of its wrapper and blew into the end. It made a terrible noise. Lou tried again, but again it made a terrible noise.

Lou probably feels —
- O   disappointed
- O   proud
- O   happy
- O   delighted

> Cory's grandfather had a terrible cold and would not be able to go on the hike they had planned. Cory wanted to do something special for his grandfather. He decided to go to the library to get a book on hiking. He brought the book home and showed it to his grandfather.
> "Cory, your kindness makes me feel so much better," Cory's grandfather said. The two smiled and gave each other a hug.

How does Cory make Grandfather feel?
- O   Glad
- O   Angry
- O   Confused
- O   Wise

Some questions on the TAAS will ask you how a character feels about doing something or going somewhere.

> Anne couldn't wait for Tim's birthday party. Tim told her that there would be movies and games and lots of fun stuff at his party.

How did Anne feel about going to Tim's birthday party?

- ○ Afraid
- ○ Delighted
- ○ Sad
- ○ Tired

Sometimes a question will ask how someone or something can be best described. Don't forget to rule out bad answer choices!

> Cassie was smiling as she woke up. She took a deep breath and bounced out of bed with one leap. She brushed her teeth, got dressed, and made the bed. Cassie was ready for her first day at school.

Cassie can be best described as —

- ○ puzzled
- ○ angry
- ○ excited
- ○ bored

> David couldn't believe the number of fish he saw in the water.

In this story, David is —

- ○ jealous
- ○ quiet
- ○ helpful
- ○ surprised

Practice: Inference and Generalization Questions

Use all of the things that you have learned so far. Label the paragraphs, look for clues, and underline the details you find.

Benga Wants to Play the Violin

Benga and his parents went to every concert in their town. Everyone in the family loved music. Benga liked violin music the best. His neighbor, Mrs. Allen, played the violin in the symphony. Sometimes she let Benga listen to her practice.

At the beginning of the school year, Benga asked his parents if he could rent a violin. He knew that he could rent one from the school. His music teacher had offered to give him violin lessons.

"Playing the violin takes lots of practice, Benga," his mother said. "You will need to practice every day if you want to know how to play."

"I'm ready to do that, Mom," Benga said. "It will be worth the hard work."

On Friday, Benga's father met him after school. They chose a violin made of dark, smooth wood.

On the way home, Benga and his father stopped at the music store. His father helped him pick out some music for <u>novices</u>. It was the right music for someone who was just learning to play the violin.

Benga could hardly wait to play his violin. He put a chair in the living room near a bright lamp. Then he opened his new music book. He looked at the pictures that showed him how to hold the violin. He tried to play but the sounds that came out of the violin were terrible! He looked at the music book some more. Then he tried to play the notes again. The sound was still terrible. Benga felt awful.

"This is harder than I thought it would be," he said to his mother.

"Why don't you call Mrs. Allen and ask her if she will help you?" his mother asked.

Benga called, and Mrs. Allen invited Benga to come over with his violin.

"To start, let me see how you hold your violin," Mrs. Allen said to Benga. She watched Benga for a few minutes. "Benga, I think that your violin is too big for you. I have a smaller one that you might like to try. It's called a three-quarter violin. I'll go find it." Soon she brought back a smaller violin.

Benga held the violin and smiled. It fit under his chin better. He could reach the notes with his fingers better. He played a few notes. It sounded just fine!

"I'll ask my father to help me trade my violin for a smaller one like this," Benga said. "Then I'll learn to play the violin as well as you do!"

1 In this story, <u>novices</u> are —

   ○ teachers

   ○ parents

   ○ musicians

   ○ beginners

2 Which one of these happened first?

   ○ Benga played the smaller violin.

   ○ Benga asked his parents for a violin.

   ○ Benga called Mrs. Allen for help.

   ○ Benga played the violin and it sounded terrible.

3 What did Benga's father do when he took him to the music store?

   ○ Stayed in the car

   ○ Picked out a violin

   ○ Played his violin

   ○ Helped him pick out music

4 In this story, Mrs. Allen is —

   ○ angry

   ○ bored

   ○ helpful

   ○ confused

5 How did Benga feel when the violin sounded terrible?

   ○ Jealous

   ○ Sad

   ○ Tired

   ○ Excited

6 How did Benga feel about playing the violin at the end of the story?

   ○ Bored

   ○ Hopeful

   ○ Lazy

   ○ Angry

7 Mrs. Allen's advice to Benga shows that she is —

   ○ jealous

   ○ boring

   ○ wise

   ○ tricky

8 When does this story take place?

   ○ At the beginning of the school year

   ○ A long time ago

   ○ Today

   ○ Last month

Practice: Inference and Generalization Questions

Use all of the things that you have learned so far. Label the paragraphs, look for clues, and underline the details you find.

Treasures in the Sand

Claire ran all of the way home from school. She was in a hurry because she was going to see her friend Eduardo. Eduardo lived on the beach. Every Tuesday the two friends went to the dunes. They played in the big hills of sand that drifted all along the water.

They had a special way of getting ready for their trip to the dunes. They put on lots of sunscreen. Then they packed two apples, two bottles of water, and a blanket in a basket. They promised each other that if they found a treasure they would share it. Then they said goodbye to Eduardo's mother and ran out the back door. This was the routine they followed every Tuesday.

When they got to the dunes, they said hello to Laura. She was the same lifeguard that had always been at the beach. Claire and Eduardo spread the blanket out on the sand. It was a hot day, so they had a drink of water. Then Claire climbed the nearest sand dune. Eduardo sat on the edge of the blanket and took off his shoes. He dug in the sand with his toes. Then he saw something shiny in the sand. Eduardo used his hands to clear away the sand.

"Claire, come here! I think I found a treasure — gold coins!" Eduardo exclaimed.

Claire ran down the sand dune and helped Eduardo dig around in the sand.

They found fifty gold coins!

"It's a pirate's treasure! They were probably lost here in a shipwreck a thousand years ago! We will be rich! Let's go home and show your mom. She can tell us how to find out how much money they are worth!" Claire said excitedly.

Claire and Eduardo put all the coins in the basket. They folded the blanket on top of the coins and ran home.

"Why are you two so excited?" asked Eduardo's mother.

"Look, we found gold coins! We are rich!" said Eduardo. He spread the coins out on the picnic table and showed his mother.

Eduardo's mother sat at the table and picked up some of the coins. Eduardo and Claire stood behind her, looking over her shoulders. She looked at the coins. Then she looked at Eduardo and Claire. The two children leaned over and she said softly, "I'm sorry, but this is not a treasure. Do you remember the carnival that was here last summer? See the words around the edge of the coins? They say Buster's Carnival. I know you thought you found something special, but these are just game tokens. I'm sorry."

"Oh, well," Claire said. She could tell that Eduardo was upset. "Maybe next week when we go back to the dunes we'll find a real treasure."

1 Where was the treasure found?

- ○ At school
- ○ In Claire's yard
- ○ In the sand
- ○ In Eduardo's yard

2 How did Claire feel about going to Eduardo's house?

- ○ Confused
- ○ Worried
- ○ Excited
- ○ Lonely

3 In this story, the word <u>dunes</u> means —

- ○ sunscreen
- ○ blanket
- ○ gold coins
- ○ hills of sand

4 The word <u>routine</u> in this story means —

- ○ the same way of doing something
- ○ a list of rules
- ○ the way to put everything in a basket
- ○ a place to eat apples

5 When did Claire and Eduardo find the treasure?

- ○ On Tuesday
- ○ Before school
- ○ Before breakfast
- ○ Late at night

6 Eduardo's mother can best be described as —

- ○ kind
- ○ hungry
- ○ funny
- ○ tricky

7 How did Eduardo probably feel when he found out that the coins were not gold?

- ○ Bored
- ○ Happy
- ○ Disappointed
- ○ Puzzled

8 What happened after the two friends discovered the coins were not gold?

- ○ They put on sunscreen.
- ○ Claire decided they would go back to the dunes next week.
- ○ They put everything in a basket.
- ○ They get apples and water.

Cause and Effect Questions and Prediction Questions

CAUSE AND EFFECT QUESTIONS

Cause and effect questions on the TAAS will ask you **why someone did something or why someone felt a certain way**. Other times, the TAAS will ask **why something happened**. The answer, or clues to help you find the answer, will always be in the story.

You need to go back to the story to find the answer to the question. Then read all the answer choices to find the best one.

Hugo stood at the edge of the baseball diamond while his mother spoke with Coach Green. It was Hugo's first day at baseball camp. He was nervous, but he was looking forward to learning how to play baseball.

Hugo watched the other kids throw the baseballs around the field. They threw the balls very hard and very far. Hugo was not sure he would be able to do that.

"Are you ready to play some baseball, Hugo?" Coach Green asked. Hugo was not sure he was ready, but he nodded bravely to Coach Green.

Hugo was nervous because —

○ the coach called his name

○ it was his first day at baseball camp

○ the baseball field was wet

○ the other kids were laughing at him

Prediction Questions

Some questions on the TAAS will ask you to figure out **what will probably happen next**, or **what someone will do next**. When you see a question like this, rule out wrong answers and place an X at the end of them. The answer will not be stated in the story. It is up to you to figure out which answer choice will *probably* happen.

Remember, the question does not ask what **you** would probably do. It asks, based on the information in the story, what the **character** in the story will probably do.

Make sure you read *all* of the answer choices and look back at the story before choosing the *best* answer.

When Hanna first learned that her family was moving to another town, she cried for three days. Every time she went out into the neighborhood, she felt sad. Soon she wouldn't see that neighborhood anymore.

Hanna's mother asked her what she would miss the most. Hanna thought about it for a long time. She would miss a lot of things. She would miss the Garcias' dogs barking behind the fence. She would miss the pretty colors Mr. Bondurant had painted his window frames. She would miss the big bushes around Ms. Keefer's house. But she decided that the thing she would miss the most was the tree house in her friend Mimi's backyard.

Because of what she will miss most, Hanna will probably try to —

○ build a tree house in her new yard

○ stay at Ms. Keefer's house

○ paint her windows

○ walk the Garcias' dog

© McGraw-Hill School Division

Practice: Cause and Effect Questions and Prediction Questions

Use all of the things that you have learned so far. Label the paragraphs, look for clues, and underline the details you find. Use the process of elimination.

Lidia's First Swim Meet

Lidia came in the back door with a frown on her face. She did not want to go to her swimming lesson tomorrow. She was glad her mother let her join the swim team. But yesterday, Mrs. Graves, the coach, said that they would start practice races on Wednesday. Tomorrow was Wednesday, and Lidia was not sure that she would be ready for the practice races. She had never raced before.

Her mother sat down next to her and said, "Lidia, what is the matter?"

"How am I going to swim with people watching me?" she asked her mother. "What if I don't race well?"

"How about if we go to the pool?" her mother asked. "Get your swimsuit. I'll get mine and then I'll meet you in the car. I'm sure it will help if we go swim for a while today."

It was late in the afternoon when they arrived at the pool and not many people were there. Lidia and her mother stood next to each other and got ready to race each other. Lidia could feel her heart pounding. Then her mother said, "On your mark! Get set! Go!"

When they hit the water, Lidia forgot all about the fact that she was in a race. She didn't worry about the people who might be watching, and she started to swim. Lidia remembered all of the things that she had learned. Her strokes were smooth and her breathing was even. She pulled her arms through the water and kicked her legs. Lidia swam quickly and strongly. She finished first. She waited for her mother to finish and then said, "That was fun, Mom! And I beat you!" Lidia smiled brightly.

"Yes, you did!" her mother said. "Do you want to race again?"

The same thing happened when Lidia dove into the water. She forgot all about the race and the people and enjoyed swimming. This time her mother finished first.

"That was fun! And this time you were the <u>champion</u>," Lidia exclaimed.

As they drove home from the pool Lidia said, "I'll be fine at swim practice, won't I?"

"Yes you will, Lidia," her mother said and they both smiled.

1 Who asked Lidia to go to the pool?

    ○ Lidia's father

    ○ Mrs. Graves

    ○ Lidia's mother

    ○ Lidia's teacher

2 Which of these happened last in the story?

    ○ Lidia came in the back door with a frown on her face.

    ○ Lidia's mother won the race.

    ○ Lidia and her mother talked on the way home.

    ○ Lidia and her mother got their swimsuits and drove to the pool.

3 Lidia's heart pounded because —

    ○ her mother asked her what was the matter

    ○ she was nervous about racing

    ○ the water was cold

    ○ there were not many people at the pool

4 Tomorrow Lidia will probably want to —

    ○ stay home

    ○ go to a different pool

    ○ have breakfast with her mother

    ○ go to her swimming practice

5 At the beginning of the story, how did Lidia feel about the practice races?

    ○ Bored

    ○ Unsure

    ○ Angry

    ○ Happy

6 Lidia did not want to go to her Wednesday swimming lesson because did not want to —

    ○ go to school

    ○ get wet

    ○ walk to the pool

    ○ practice racing

7 The word <u>champion</u> in this story means —

    ○ winner

    ○ swimmer

    ○ coach

    ○ diver

8 How did Lidia feel when she won the race against her mother?

    ○ Bored

    ○ Sad

    ○ Disappointed

    ○ Happy

Practice: Cause and Effect Questions and Prediction Answers

Use all of the things that you have learned so far. Label the paragraphs, look for clues, and underline the details you find. Use the process of elimination.

Grandma's Note to Marsell

Marsell was glad it was summer. He enjoyed helping his Grandma Marie in her garden during the warm summer months. Grandma Marie's garden was large and it needed lots of attention every week. This week, Grandma would not be home. She wrote Marsell a note that provided him with <u>instructions</u> about how to care for the garden. It told him what to do with each plant.

Dear Marsell,

I'm sorry that I won't see you this week. I hope that this isn't too much work for you to finish in one day. If you get tired, take a break on the back porch. I left you a bottle of water and some fruit.

Tomatoes: It has been extra hot this week, so give them plenty of water. I know that tomatoes are your brother's favorite so I put one of the plants in a small pot. Please take it home with you and give it to him.

Peas: We didn't get many peas last year, remember? They just didn't grow well. Maybe a little fertilizer will help this year. Sprinkle some around each plant.

Carrots: The carrots will grow anywhere. Please pull up all of the carrots that have sprouted outside of the row.

Rhubarb: Please cut all of the stalks that are deep purple. They are ripe. You can put them in a plastic bag and put them in the refrigerator.

Beans: There are lots of weeds around the beans. The weeds will choke the beans out if they are not taken care of. Sometimes it is hard to tell which is the weed and which is the bean plant. Be sure you pull up the right ones!

Thank you so much for all of your assistance. You are a wonderful helper. See you next week.

Love, Grandma Marie

1   The word <u>instructions</u> in this story means —

○   a list of things to do

○   the names of all the plants

○   a large garden

○   a set of tools

2   According to the note, Grandma Marie's garden does **NOT** have any —

○   tomatoes

○   corn

○   carrots

○   beans

3   Grandma Marie's note shows that she is —

○   curious

○   bored

○   caring

○   angry

4   A tomato plant will be sent home to Marsell's brother because he —

○   is sick

○   wants to give it to his sister

○   asked for a tomato plant

○   likes tomatoes

5   At the beginning of the story, Marsell feels —

○   hungry

○   lazy

○   curious

○   glad

6   Why does Marsell like to help Grandma Marie in the summer?

○   He likes to eat lunch.

○   He wants to make money.

○   He likes to work in her garden.

○   He wants some fruit.

7   A little fertilizer is put on the peas because they —

○   are green

○   are growing too fast

○   are too hot

○   did not grow well last year

8   When does this story take place?

○   In the summer

○   After school

○   Last year

○   Tomorrow

Fact, Opinion, and Make-Believe Questions

WHAT IS A FACT?

Some questions on the TAAS will ask you, "Which of these is a FACT in the story?" For a question like this, only *one* answer choice will be **a fact that you can find in the story**. It is important that you go back to the story to see if the answer choice matches the story.

Pocahontas was a Native American princess. People who study history believe that she was born in about 1595 in the part of America that is now the state of Virginia. When she was born, she was named Matoaka. She later earned the name Pocahontas, which means "playful one."

When Pocahontas was about seventeen years old, she moved to Jamestown, Virginia. There she helped to keep the peace between the Native Americans and the early Jamestown settlers. She married John Rolfe, a man from Jamestown, in 1614.

In this story, which of these is a FACT?

- O Matoaka was Pocahontas' mother.
- O Pocahontas lived in Jamestown.
- O Pocahontas enjoyed being a princess.
- O John Rolfe liked Pocahontas a lot.

You may not be sure which answer choice is *best* right away, but you can put an X at the end of answers that you know are wrong. Remember the FACT will be in the story.

In this story, which of these is a FACT?

- Matoaka was Pocahontas' mother.

Is this a fact? No. Look at the story. When Pocahontas was born she was named Matoaka. Put an X after the answer choice.

- Pocahontas lived in Jamestown.

Is this a fact? Yes. This was stated in the story. Check the other answer choices to be sure.

- Pocahontas enjoyed being a princess.

Is this a fact? No. This may be true, but it was never stated in the story. The story said she *was* a princess — not that she enjoyed being one. Put an X after the answer choice.

- John Rolfe liked Pocahontas a lot.

Is this a fact? No. It may be true, but it is NOT a fact from the story. It was never stated in the story that John Rolfe liked Pocahontas. Put an X after the answer choice.

WHAT IS NOT A FACT?

When a question asks, "Which of these is **NOT** a fact?" there will be only *one* answer that is **NOT** a fact that is stated in the story. **All the other answer choices will be facts that you can find in the story**. Make sure you read all of the answer choices. Then, look back at the story before choosing the best answer.

Brandi talked to her gym teacher, Mr. Malcolm, about playing soccer over the summer. Mr. Malcolm ran the summer soccer club. He knew that Brandi loved to play soccer and he said that he'd enjoy having Brandi play on the team. Brandi's favorite position was halfback. She liked that position because a halfback ran a lot.

Which of these is **NOT** a fact from the story?
- ○ Brandi's favorite position was halfback.
- ○ Brandi talked to her gym teacher.
- ○ Mr. Malcolm ran the summer soccer club.
- ○ Soccer was Brandi's favorite sport.

The best way to make sure you do well on these questions is to eliminate answers that you know are wrong by placing an X after them.

Which of these is **NOT** a fact from the story?

• Brandi's favorite position was halfback.	Is this a fact? Yes. This was stated in the story. This **is** a fact, so it cannot be the correct answer. Put an X after the answer choice.
• Brandi talked to her gym teacher.	Is this a fact? Yes. This was stated in the story. This **is** a fact, so it cannot be the correct answer. Put an X after the answer choice.
• Mr. Malcolm ran the summer soccer club.	Is this a fact? Yes. This was stated in the story. This **is** a fact, so it cannot be the correct answer. Put an X after the answer choice.
• Soccer was Brandi's favorite sport.	Is this a fact? No. It may be true, but it is *not a fact* from the story. It was never stated in the story that soccer was Brandi's favorite sport. So it must be the correct answer. Fill in the answer bubble.

WHAT IS AN OPINION?

An OPINION is different from a fact. An OPINION is something that is usually based on feelings that someone has. Some questions will ask you to determine which answer choice is an OPINION.

> Brad and Wendy went to the local craft store with the money from their piggy banks. With their money, they bought construction paper, glue, and a small pair of scissors. They brought the things home and they made the most beautiful birthday card they had ever seen! Inside the card, it said in big red letters: "Happy Birthday, Grandma!"

Which of these is an OPINION from the story?

○ The card was for their grandmother's birthday.
○ Brad and Wendy spent the money from their piggy banks.
○ The birthday card was the most beautiful card they had ever seen.
○ Brad and Wendy found it hard to wait until grandmother's birthday.

Let's rule out wrong answers to help us find the best answer more easily.

Which of these is an OPINION from the story?

- The card was for their grandmother's birthday.

Does this answer choice show how *someone feels* about something in the story? No. This is a fact from the story. In this case we do not want a fact, but an opinion. Put an X after the answer choice.

- Brad and Wendy spent the money from their piggy banks.

Does this answer choice show how *someone feels* about something in the story? No. This is a fact from the story. Put an X after the answer choice.

- The birthday card was the most beautiful card they had ever seen.

Does this answer choice show how *someone feels* about something in the story? Yes. Brad and Wendy *feel* that this is the *most beautiful* card they have ever seen. Check the last answer choice to be sure.

- Brad and Wendy found it hard to wait until grandmother's birthday.

Does this answer choice show how *someone feels* about something in the story? Well, it is an opinion—but wait. Remember that the best answer is something *from the story*. This is not an opinion *in this story*. Put an X after the answer choice.

WHAT CAN REALLY HAPPEN?

Sometimes a question on the TAAS will ask you which thing could have *REALLY* happened. When you see a question like this, the *best* answer choice will be the *only* thing that can happen in *real* life. The wrong answer choices will all be make-believe. They will be things that cannot happen in real life.

> Ralph looked at two puppies that seemed to need a lot of attention. One was a very big floppy puppy with large ears and a big tail that wagged. The other was a small puppy with a pink nose. The puppies were very playful. They tugged on each other's ears and licked Ralph's face.

Which one of these could have REALLY happened?

- ○ Ralph played with two puppies.
- ○ One puppy had ears as big as a house.
- ○ One puppy weighed more than a car.
- ○ Ralph was ten feet tall.

Let's rule out the answers that cannot happen in real life.

Which one of these could have REALLY happened?

• Ralph played with two puppies.	Could this really happen in real life? Yes. This could be the best answer. Check the other answer choices to be sure.
• One puppy had ears as big as a house.	Could this really happen in real life? No. This could <u>not</u> REALLY happen. Put an X after the answer choice.
• One puppy weighed more than a car.	Could this really happen in real life? No. This could <u>not</u> REALLY happen. Put an X after the answer choice.
• Ralph was ten feet tall.	Could this really happen in real life? No. This could <u>not</u> REALLY happen. Put an X after the answer choice.

WHAT IS MAKE-BELIEVE?

Other times, a question on the TAAS will ask you how you can tell that a story is *make-believe*. When you see a question like that, the *best* answer choice will be the only thing that *cannot* happen in real life. The wrong answer choices will all be possible—they will be things that can happen.

> Three little robin's eggs hatched one day in a nest. The nest was high up in a tree. The mama robin looked at her newborn chicks with pride. She had been waiting for them to hatch for a very long time!
>
> One chick said, "When can I fly?"
>
> "Flying will come naturally to you," the mother robin said. "You can fly whenever you spread your wings."

You know this story is make-believe because —

- ○ birds do not live in nests
- ○ birds cannot talk
- ○ birds do not hatch from eggs
- ○ birds cannot fly

Let's rule out the answers that **can** happen in real life.

You know this story is make-believe because —

- birds do not live in nests

Is this make-believe? No. Birds really do live in nests. This cannot be the *best* answer because it is **not** make-believe. Put an X after the answer choice.

- birds cannot talk

Is this make-believe? Yes. Birds can't talk! This could be the *best* answer. Check the other answer choices to be sure.

- birds do not hatch from eggs

Is this make-believe? No. Birds really do hatch from eggs. This cannot be the *best* answer because it is **not** make-believe. Put an X after the answer choice.

- birds cannot fly

Is this make-believe? No. Birds really do fly. This cannot be the *best* answer because it is **not** make-believe. Put an X after the answer choice.

Practice: Fact, Opinion, and Make-Believe Questions

Use all of the things that you have learned so far. Label the paragraphs, look for clues, and underline the details you find. Use the process of elimination.

The People's Choice

Cars are displayed for people to enjoy at many car shows around the country. Different contests are held to pick the best car in a few categories. Often, the people who attend the car show are asked to pick their favorite. Their overall favorite is called "The People's Choice."

During the car show, the cars are parked so people can get a good look at them. The cars are not driven around but are parked in rows. They are usually placed by the ages of the cars. Owners put a sign on or near their car that tells important facts about the car. Sometimes the sign tells how big the engine is. Sometimes it tells how many miles the car has been driven. The owners stay with their cars. They answer questions about the car.

There were three contests at the car show last summer. One was to find the car that had the best paint job. To choose the winner, the judges looked at how smooth and shiny the paint was. Some of the cars had fancy paint jobs. Others even had pictures painted on them. The car that won last summer was bright orange. It had a giant spider web painted on it. The spider was painted on the roof of the car.

Another contest last summer was for the car that was the most <u>customized</u>.

That was the car that was changed the most from how it looked when it was first made. The judges looked at the car inside and out in order to choose the winner. They looked at all of the changes that were made. Then they looked at photos of what the car looked like before the changes were made. The car that won last summer looked more like a boat than a car!

The contest that was the most fun was the one when people who visited the car show got to choose their favorite car. Each person wrote the license number of the car that they liked best on a piece of paper. Then they dropped the paper into a box. The judges counted the number of votes for each car. The car that received the most votes was a purple racecar with a yellow lightning bolt on it. The owner of the car won a trophy that said, "The People's Choice!"

1 In this story, the word underline{customized} means —
  ○ broken
  ○ changed
  ○ washed
  ○ polished

2 What happens when a car wins *The People's Choice* contest?
  ○ The owner answers questions.
  ○ The owner receives a trophy.
  ○ The owner parks the car and stands beside it.
  ○ The owner keeps the car clean.

3 Which is a FACT in the story?
  ○ The car with the best paint job is called *The People's Choice*.
  ○ The judges choose the car with the best paint job.
  ○ Owners don't like being in car shows.
  ○ Big cars usually win a prize.

4 What is one of the jobs of a judge at a car show?
  ○ To make a sign with facts about the car
  ○ To answer questions about the car
  ○ To look at the car inside and out
  ○ To keep the car clean and shiny

5 The winner of *The People's Choice* trophy will probably want to —
  ○ paint the car
  ○ enter more car shows
  ○ ride the bus
  ○ write a book

6 The winner of *The People's Choice* trophy probably feels —
  ○ unhappy
  ○ proud
  ○ jealous
  ○ confused

7 Which of these is **NOT** a fact from the story?
  ○ The cars are not driven around at the show.
  ○ The owners sell their cars before they go home.
  ○ There were three contests at last summer's show.
  ○ The people pick their favorite car.

8 Which one of these could have REALLY happened?
  ○ The owners brought their cars to the car show.
  ○ One owner had a car made out of spider webs.
  ○ One car floated like a boat.
  ○ One car was as big as a school.

Practice: Fact, Opinion, and Make-Believe Questions

Use all of the things that you have learned so far. Label the paragraphs, look for clues, and underline the details you find. Use the process of elimination.

Carla's Surprise

Rita was very happy when school was over for the week. She was going to spend the night at Carla's house. Carla's father had promised they could look through all of the old trunks in the basement.

After breakfast Saturday morning, the girls helped Carla's father wash the dishes and clean up the kitchen. Then they raced down the stairs to the basement. They moved two chairs and an old lamp out of the way. Then they put an old blanket on the floor and opened the trunk.

There were wonderful items in the trunk. There were some old hats. There was a pair of old shoes and a shirt that looked like it had belonged to a sailor. Carla opened a small wooden case. It was full of earrings. Underneath the case, an old doll lay on top of a pile of pillowcases. At the very bottom of the trunk there were two silk dresses. They were old fashioned with lots of lace and bows. There were also two pair of shoes that matched the dresses.

"Look, Rita. These must have belonged to my great-grandmother!" Carla exclaimed.

"Do you think we can try them on?" Rita asked.

The girls quickly <u>gathered</u> all of the things together and rushed upstairs to Carla's bedroom. The girls tried on the dresses and shoes. Then they put on the earrings and the hats.

Rita said, "Wow! You look like a famous movie star." Rita could not believe how gorgeous Carla looked in the dress. "How do I look?" she asked.

"You look terrific!" said Carla as she twirled around in her dress. "Let's go show my father. He never mentioned that we had such interesting things in that trunk," Carla said.

The girls went into the study where Carla's father was reading. Carla said, "Look, Dad. I bet you didn't know that you had two famous movie stars in your house."

Carla's father looked up and smiled. "Those dresses belonged to my grandmother. I haven't seen them in years. They certainly look lovely on you two. Would you like me to take your picture?" he asked.

1 How did Rita feel about going to Carla's house?
- ○ Worried
- ○ Calm
- ○ Happy
- ○ Bored

2 Where was the trunk?
- ○ In the back yard
- ○ At the store
- ○ In Carla's basement
- ○ In Rita's house

3 In this story, the word <u>gathered</u> means —
- ○ thought about
- ○ looked at
- ○ listened to
- ○ picked up

4 When did Carla and Rita find the dresses?
- ○ On Saturday
- ○ During the week
- ○ At night
- ○ Friday morning

5 What will the girls probably do next?
- ○ Go to the store
- ○ Get their picture taken
- ○ Watch television
- ○ Eat cookies

6 Which of these is **NOT** a fact in the story?
- ○ Carla opened a small wooden case.
- ○ Carla and Rita found a sailor in the basement.
- ○ Carla and Rita moved chairs out of the way.
- ○ Carla and Rita tried on dresses.

7 Which one of these could have REALLY happened?
- ○ Rita and Carla found a hat.
- ○ One of the chairs danced.
- ○ The doll talked to Rita and Carla.
- ○ The trunk was bigger than the house.

8 Which of these happened last in the story?
- ○ Rita found a wooden case full of earrings.
- ○ Carla's dad said the dresses looked lovely on the girls.
- ○ Rita and Carla helped clean up the kitchen.
- ○ Rita and Carla raced down the stairs to the basement.

"Mostly about" and Main Idea Questions

When you are trying to figure out what a story on the TAAS is *mostly about*, look back at the story. Look at the labels you wrote next to the paragraphs. Look at the words you underlined in the story. All of these will tell you what the story is *mostly about*.

This kind of question will be asked in one of two ways: "What is the story mostly about?" Or, less often, "What is the main idea of the story?"

What does this story talk about most? Don't forget to label!

Rachel and her father were walking home from the store. They saw a man at the crosswalk dressed in a clown outfit. The clown was scratching his head and looking puzzled. Rachel and her father walked up to him and said hello.

"Hello," said the clown. "I'm Bubbles the Clown." He honked his nose. HONK! HONK!

"Is there something wrong?" Rachel's father asked.

Bubbles frowned. "I think I'm lost," he said. "I've got to get to the circus in an hour or I'll miss the show." He honked his nose again.

Rachel smiled. " We went to the circus last night. We know exactly where it is," she said. "Dad will give you directions!"

This story is mostly about —

- ○ walking home from the store
- ○ a clown who was lost
- ○ being late for the circus
- ○ Rachel's father

When you are trying to figure out what the *main idea* of a story on the TAAS is, look back at the story. Ask yourself, "What was this story *mainly* about?" What is the story trying to tell you? Sometimes a question about a main idea will be asking you to find the answer that tells the message or the lesson of the story.

What does this story talk about *most*? Don't forget to label.

> Most of the time, farmers are glad that it snows. In the winter the snow falls in the mountains. Then in the spring, the snow melts and fills up the lakes and rivers with fresh water. This gives farmers water for their crops. Where there are no mountains, lakes, or rivers, the snow melts and runs down through the dirt. It goes far down underground. Farmers use wells to get the water out of the ground. Then the farmers can use the well water for their fields.

This question tells you that the main idea of the story has something to do with *farmers*. Look back at the story. What did the story say about *farmers*?

The main idea of this story is that farmers —

- ○ are not important
- ○ are glad when it snows
- ○ swim in rivers
- ○ like the summer

Practice: "Mostly about" and Main Idea Questions

Use all of the things that you have learned so far. Label the paragraphs, look for clues, and underline the details you find. Use the process of elimination.

What did we do before television?

Today, there is a television in almost all of the homes in the United States. But, the television is not an old invention. It has only been around for about fifty years. Children had to find other things to do for fun before the television was invented. Sometimes children told stories or played games together. Other times, children learned new hobbies. Often, families listened to the radio or read stories out loud in the evening.

Many families had a lot of people in them. It was common for grandparents, parents, and children to all live together. And, there was almost always an adult nearby who would play with the children or would tell them a story.

Most homes that were out in the country had animals. Children spent lots of time with their animals. They rode their horses and took care of their chickens. They milked the cows and played in the hay. In the summer, they swam in the creeks. When there was extra wood around, they built tree houses. Children learned how to make toys out of wood. They also learned how to make dolls out of socks. They had plenty of time to play even though they had chores to do.

People told stories when they lived far from a library and could not get books. Sometimes the stories were true. Other times they were "tall tales," or make-believe stories. Grandparents often told stories of how different life was when they were young.

Some families were lucky enough to have musical instruments and someone who knew how to play them. They would have their own <u>performance</u>. Even without instruments, everyone could always sing.

There were lots of fun things to do before television was invented. You can still do most of them today!

1 In this story, a <u>performance</u> is a —

    ◯ good book

    ◯ drawing

    ◯ music concert

    ◯ story

2 Which of these is NOT a fact from the story?

    ◯ Children learned how to make dolls.

    ◯ Fathers worked in libraries.

    ◯ People told stories.

    ◯ Children took care of the chickens.

3 What is this story mostly about?

    ◯ What stories grandparents like to tell

    ◯ How to make a doll out of a sock

    ◯ How people had fun before television

    ◯ Where children liked to swim

4 People made up stories to tell each other because —

    ◯ they liked to swim in the creek

    ◯ it was hard to play musical instruments

    ◯ they were not taught how to make dolls

    ◯ it could be difficult to get books

Practice: "Mostly about" and Main Idea Questions

Use all of the things that you have learned so far. Label the paragraphs, look for clues, and underline the details you find. Use the process of elimination.

What will Sidney choose for her bedroom?

Sidney was walking out the door of the library with her cousin Morgan. They walked past the bulletin board and saw this sign.

Free Decorating Tips!
Change the Color of Your Walls!
Call Ms. Grove at 555-8236

"I have a great idea!" Sidney said. "Let's ask my dad if we can paint my bedroom a different color."

When they got to Sidney's house, Sidney and Morgan got some magazines off the bookshelf. Sidney's father was an interior decorator, and he designed bedrooms and living rooms for all kinds of people's homes. They sat in the kitchen and looked through the magazines for some ideas.

"What are you girls up to?" Sidney's father asked.

"I want to paint my bedroom a different color. I was thinking that <u>enormous</u> green polka dots would look neat." Sidney loved polka dots and she thought that the bigger they were, the better they were. "What do you think, can I do it? Morgan says that she will help me and we won't make a mess," Sidney said.

Sidney's father sat on the couch. He knew how much Sidney liked polka dots but he wasn't sure that giant green dots would look good in her bedroom. He said, "Yes, you can paint your room. I'll have some free time this weekend and I can help you, too. Do you really think that you want green polka dots, though?"

Sidney and Morgan said that they would look at more pictures before they made a choice. First, they looked at a picture of a room that was all green. It was a dark green and it reminded Morgan of the grass in springtime. Sidney thought that a plain green room might be too boring. And, she wasn't sure that she would be happy with it.

Next they looked at a room that was red and white. The walls were striped and the furniture was painted a glossy red. Morgan liked it a lot but Sidney thought that it would make her dizzy if she had to look at it every day.

Then Morgan pointed out a picture of a room that was a light yellow with darker yellow polka dots on the walls. Sidney thought it looked cheerful and sunny. Sidney smiled. She said, "Let's show this picture to my dad, I think that he'll like it, too. It will brighten up my room and it will have polka dots!"

1 Where does this story mostly take place?

   ○ At the library

   ○ At school

   ○ Sidney's house

   ○ Ms. Grove's house

2 Which is a FACT in the story?

   ○ Sidney's father has too many magazines.

   ○ Sidney's father looked through the magazines for ideas.

   ○ Sidney's father said that he would help her paint her room.

   ○ Morgan liked to paint.

3 Why did Sidney choose the color yellow?

   ○ It was the only color she could have.

   ○ She thought it would be cheerful and sunny.

   ○ Ms. Grove said it was the best color.

   ○ Sidney's father liked it the best.

4 In this story, the word <u>enormous</u> means —

   ○ large

   ○ old

   ○ bright

   ○ heavy

5 Where did Sidney's father keep the magazines?

   ○ On the bookshelf

   ○ In the yard

   ○ In a box

   ○ On the desk

6 This story is mostly about how Sidney —

   ○ likes to go to the library

   ○ saw a sign on the bulletin board

   ○ decided to paint the walls in her room

   ○ started painting right away

7 The main idea of this story is that Sidney —

   ○ likes to read

   ○ makes a decision

   ○ walks home with Morgan

   ○ wants to look at magazines